10 Minute Guide to
Microsoft® Windows™ 3

Katherine Murray
Doug Sabotin

A Division of Macmillan Computer Publishing
11711 North College, Carmel, Indiana 46032 USA

Katie...
Know the Truth and the Truth Shall Set You Free
Thank You...

International Standard Book Number: 0-672-22812-2
Library of Congress Catalog Card Number: 90-72143

Acquisitions Editor: *Marie Butler-Knight*
Book Design: *Dan Armstrong, reVisions Plus, Inc.*
Manuscript Editors: *Ronda Henry and Charles Hutchinson*
Cover Design: *Dan Armstrong*
Production: *reVisions Plus, Inc.*
Indexer: *Katherine Murray*
Technical Reviewer: *San Dee Phillips*

Printed in the United States of America.

Trademarks

All terms mentioned in this book that are known to be trademarks or service marks are listed below. In addition, terms suspected are capitalized. SAMS cannot attest to the accuracy of this information. Use of a term in this book should not be regarded as affecting the validity of any trademark or service mark.

Aldus and PageMaker are registered trademarks of Aldus Corporation.

Microsoft Windows, Microsoft Write, and Microsoft Paintbrush are registered trademarks of Microsoft Corporation.

Contents

Introduction

Perhaps you walked into work this morning and found a Microsoft Windows package sitting beside your computer, along with a mouse that wasn't there yesterday. Until now, all you've heard about Windows was that it is a program that allows users to do several tasks at once.

A few things are certain:

- You need some method of finding your way around Windows quickly and easily.

- You need to identify and learn the tasks necessary to accomplish your particular needs.

- You need some clear-cut, plain-English help to learn the basic features of the program.

Welcome to the *10 Minute Guide to Microsoft Windows 3*.

Because most people don't have the luxury of sitting down uninterrupted for hours at a time to learn a new program, the *10 Minute Guide* teaches the operations you need in lessons that can be completed in 10 minutes or less. Not only does the 10-minute format offer information in bite-sized, easy-to-follow modules, it lets you stop and start as often as you like because each lesson is a self-contained series of steps related to a particular task.

1

What Is the 10 Minute Guide?

The *10 Minute Guide* is a new approach to learning computer programs. Instead of trying to teach you *everything* about a particular software product (and ending up with an 800-page book in the process), the *10 Minute Guide* teaches you only about the most often-used features. Each *10 Minute Guide* contains between 20 and 30 short lessons.

The *10 Minute Guide* teaches you about programs without relying on computerese or technical jargon—you'll find only simple English used to explain the procedures in this book. With straightforward, easy-to-follow steps, and special art-work, called *icons*, to call your attention to important tips and definitions, the *10 Minute Guide* makes learning a new software program quick and easy.

The following icons help you find your way around in the *10 Minute Guide to Windows 3:*

 *Timesaver Tips* offering short–cuts and hints for using the program more effectively

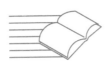 *Plain English* definitions of new terms

 *Panic Button* problem areas—how to identify them and how to solve them

Additionally, a table of features is included at the end of the book, providing you with a quick guide to Windows features that are not given full coverage in this book.

Specific conventions are used to help you find your way around Windows as easily as possible:

Numbered steps	Step-by-step instructions are highlighted so that you can easily find the procedures you need to perform basic Windows operations.
What you type	Within these numbered steps, the keys you press and the information you type are printed in a second color.
Menu names	The names of menus, commands, buttons, and dialog boxes are shown with the first letter capitalized for easy recognition.
Menu selections	Within the numbered steps, the options you select from the Windows menus are also printed in a second color.

The *10-Minute Guide to Microsoft Windows* is organized in 22 lessons, ranging from basic startup to more advanced file management and windowing features. Remember, however, that nothing in this book is *difficult*. Most users want to start at the beginning of the book with the lesson on starting Windows, and progress (as time allows) through the lessons sequentially.

Who Should Use the *10 Minute Guide to Microsoft Windows 3*?

The *10 Minute Guide to Microsoft Windows 3* is for anyone who

- Needs to learn Windows quickly

- Doesn't have a lot of time to spend learning a new program

- Feels overwhelmed by the complexity of the Windows program

- Is reluctant to learn a new program

- Wants to find out quickly whether Windows will meet his or her computer needs

- Wants a clear, concise guide to the most important features of the Windows program

What Is Microsoft Windows?

Windows helps you organize your work by allowing you to run several different programs simultaneously. Each program runs in its own separate part of the screen, or window. You can, for example, work with a letter, a spreadsheet, and a database at the same time, copying and moving information between programs, and saving and printing files from each of the programs. Windows saves you the time and trouble of having to exit one program before you load another. It also gives you the added flexibility of using a mouse to navigate your way through a program's menus and commands.

Windows also includes several accessory features that help you be more productive with your work. Included with the program are a word processor (Windows Write), a graphics program (Windows Paintbrush), and a communications utility (Windows Terminal). You also have the option of using several handy desk accessories, such as the calendar, calculator, or notepad.

For Further Reference...

There are two books about Windows that you may want to use after you complete the *10 Minute Guide to Microsoft Windows 3*:

The First Book of MicroSoft Windows 3 by Jack Nimersheim

The Best Book of MicroSoft Windows 3 by Carl Townsend

Starting Windows

In this lesson, you'll start a typical Windows session. You also learn to use the mouse and keyboard to move around the opening Windows screen.

Starting Windows

To start Windows, follow these steps:

1. Type **C:** or the letter of the drive where Windows is installed, and then press Enter.

2. Type **WIN**, and then press Enter.

You will see the Windows title screen, and then an opening screen that includes the Program Manager window and the Main window (see Figure 1-1). The Program Manager lets you organize and run the different programs that you use with Windows. The Main window contains the File Manager, DOS Prompt, Control Panel, Print Manager, Windows Setup, and Clipboard. These utilities help you use the different window functions. Later lessons explain each utility in more detail.

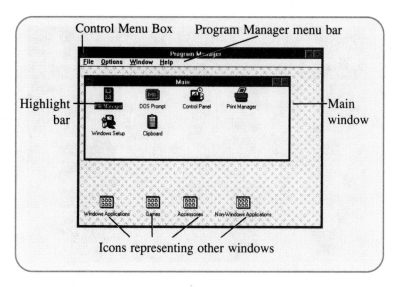

Figure 1-1. The Program Manager and Main windows in the opening screen.

If Windows is already installed on your system, your opening screen may look different. You may have a different set of utilities or the Program Manager may appear as an icon (see Figure 1-2). To display the full Program Manager window, move the mouse pointer to the icon and press the left mouse button twice in rapid succession.

Following are some basic terms you'll see often in Windows:

icon	A small picture representing a window or program you can work with in Windows
window	The basic work area in which you work with files and applications
button	A small icon that mouse users can click on to select an option

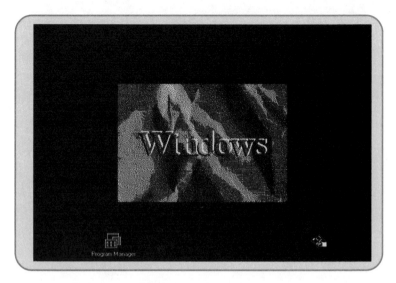

Figure 1-2. Opening screen with Program Manager reduced to an icon.

Startup Doesn't Work If Windows doesn't start when you follow these steps, you may need to change to the directory where Windows is located. This directory is named WINDOWS, unless you gave it a different name during installation. To change to it, type **CD WINDOWS** and press Enter. Then type **WIN** and press Enter.

Moving Around the Screen

You can use either a mouse or the keyboard to navigate through Windows and select commands. Throughout the next few lessons, you will find general instructions on using both. After that, instructions focus on the mouse, because that is what most people use with Windows 3.

Using a Mouse

To move around the screen using a mouse, simply move the mouse on your desk or mouse pad. You don't have to move it far or fast. When you move the mouse in any direction, the mouse pointer moves in the same direction on the screen.

If you are a new mouse user, you need to learn a few terms that are used frequently in mouse instructions:

Point	Move the mouse pointer until it touches an item.
Click	Press the left mouse button. When you are told to click on an item, first point to the item, and then press the mouse button. Clicking selects an item or command.
Double-click	Press the left button twice in quick succession. An hourglass will appear before the program appears. When told to double-click on an item, first point to the item, and then press the mouse button twice. Double-clicking selects and starts a command.
Drag	Hold down the left button and move the mouse.

Using the Keyboard

When you use the keyboard to move around the opening screen, you move from item to item. A highlight bar (see Figure 1-1) on the description below an item shows that the item is selected. You use the following keys to move the highlight bar:

Arrow keys	Move the highlight bar to the next item within the same window. Press the right arrow key to move right, and so on.
Ctrl+Tab	Press Ctrl and Tab together to move the highlight bar to the next window. The bar will move to the first item in that window.

In this lesson, you learned to start Windows. In the next lesson you will explore a basic Windows screen.

Lesson 2

Exploring
Windows

In this lesson, you'll learn about the elements of the Windows screen and explore a basic window.

Introducing the Windows Screen

One of the biggest benefits of Windows is that all the windows you see are basically the same. All the windows displayed while you are running Windows and Windows-supported applications have basically the same elements (see Figure 2-1).The selection cursor does not appear in this figure.

Table 2-1 explains each of the items in the Windows screen. Each item listed in Table 2-1 is shown in Figure 2-1. Later in this lesson, you'll practice using several of these elements.

Table 2-1. Elements in the Windows Screen

Item	Function
Title bar	Displays the name of the window and the current file name
Control-menu box	Opens the Control menu, which contains options for moving, resizing, and switching among windows

11

Table 2-1.(continued)

Item	Function
Minimize button	Reduces current window to an icon
Maximize button	Enlarges current window to fill the screen
Menu bar	Contains pull-down menus
Vertical scroll bar	Allows you to move the display up and down through current window
Horizontal scroll bar	Allows you to move the display right and left through current window
Mouse pointer	Lets you open menus, select commands, and perform other operations
Selection cursor	Shows the place on-screen where the text you type will be inserted

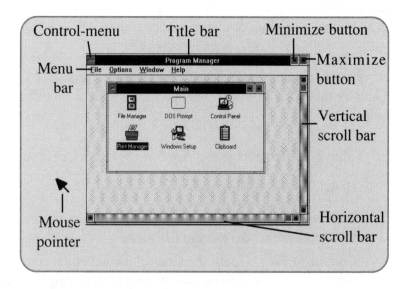

Figure 2-1. A basic window.

Note: The scroll bars display only if there are icons in the window that do not fit in the current display. If the window is open so that all icons are displayed, Windows won't display any scroll bars.

Exploring a Window

This section allows you to get familiar with the Windows screen. For this example, we'll use the Program Manager screen.

Opening and Closing the Control Menu

You use the Control menu to control the way the current window is displayed. Options in the Control menu allow you to restore, move, size, minimize, maximize, or close windows or switch to another window. (The **Restore** option is available only if you have previously modified the current window.)

To display the Control menu using the mouse,

1. Move the mouse pointer to the Control-menu box (refer to Figure 2-1).

2. Click the left mouse button.

To close the Control menu with the mouse,

1. Move the mouse pointer off the displayed menu.

2. Click the mouse button.

To display the Control menu by using the keyboard,

● Press Alt+space bar.

To close the Control menu,

● Press Esc.

Using the Scroll Bars

Other Windows elements you'll use frequently are the scroll bars. You use the scroll bars, located along the bottom and right edges of the screen, to display different parts of the current window. You can use this method of displaying windows only if you are using a mouse. (You'll use the PgUp, PgDn, and left- and right-arrow keys within applications to scroll the display from the keyboard.)

When using the scroll bars, you can click on the arrows at either end of the bar to move the display a short distance, or you can position the mouse pointer at the place in the scroll bar relative to the part of the window you want to display. For example, if you want to move to the middle of the window,

1. Position the mouse pointer in the middle of the vertical scroll bar (along the right edge of the window).

2. Click the mouse button.

Windows moves the display so that the middle portion of the window is displayed.

What If You Don't Have Any Scroll Bars? If the current window does not display any scroll bars, the window is open so that all icons are displayed. To display the scroll bars, make the window smaller by positioning the mouse pointer in the bottom right corner. Press and hold the mouse button, and, when the pointer changes to a double-sided arrow, drag the mouse up and to the left, shrinking the size of the window.

To move the display to the right in smaller increments,

- Click the arrow at the right side of the horizontal scroll bar (at the bottom of the window).

The display moves to the right.

In this lesson, you learned about the Windows screen. You also worked with several different screen elements. The next lesson shows you how to select menus and commands in Windows.

Working with Menus and Commands

In this lesson, you'll learn how to choose and cancel menus and commands and exit Windows.

Commands are the instructions that tell Windows how to carry out such operations as saving a file or running a program. Menus located in the menu bar at the top of every Windows screen group similar commands together so that you can find them easily. For example, in the Program Manager, you'll find all the commands that deal with files (such as Open, Move, Copy, and Delete) in the File menu.

Opening and Closing a Menu

Use the following procedures to open and close a menu.

If you are using a mouse:

1. Point to the menu name you want and click the mouse button. For example, click on File to display the File menu shown in Figure 3-1.

2. Move the mouse to another item or back into the work area. Click the left mouse button again to close the menu.

If you are using the keyboard:

1. Press and release the Alt key on the keyboard. This activates the menu bar at the top of the screen. File is highlighted.

2. Press the right- and left-arrow keys to highlight other menu names and return to File.

3. Press Enter to open the menu.

4. Press Alt or Esc to close the menu.

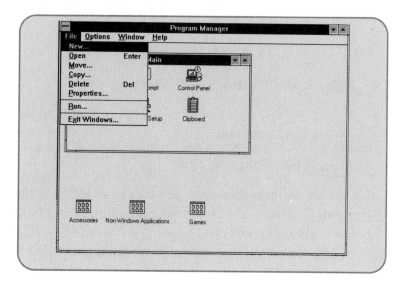

Figure 3-1. The File menu.

Selecting Menus Quickly If you're using the keyboard, you can select the menu by typing Alt plus the underlined letter of the menu name.

Choosing a Command Within a Menu

After you choose the menu you need, select a command within it using the following procedures.

If you are using a mouse:

● Point to the command you want and click the mouse button.(Do not try this until you are ready to execute a command.)

If you are using the keyboard:

1. Use the up- and down-arrow keys to highlight the command you want, or type the underlined letter for that command.

2. Press Enter.(Do not try this until you are ready to execute a command.)

Try a keyboard exercise.

1. Press Alt+F to display the File menu.

2. Use the up- and down-arrow keys to highlight the command you want.

3. Press Esc. The menu closes.

After the menu is displayed, pay special attention to the commands available. If a command is highlighted in black, this is an option that you can choose. If a command is high-lighted in gray, you cannot select it. An example of this is shown in Figure 3-2.

Windows also has a set of shortcut keys you can use to carry out a variety of operations. (These keys are listed later in this book.) Shortcut keys are key combinations that require you to press Alt, Shift, or Ctrl and a letter key. Sometimes you must press a function key with Alt, Shift, or Ctrl or press the function key alone. Try a shortcut key using the following example.

1. Press Alt+F4 (File Exit). Windows displays the End Session dialog box, asking whether you want to save changes and exit.

2. Press Tab to move the highlight from OK to Cancel.

3. Press Enter.

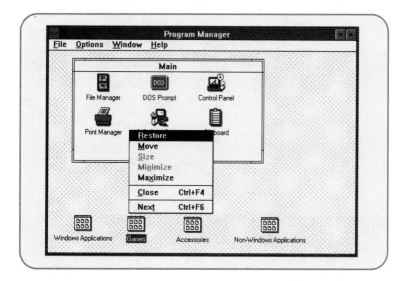

Figure 3-2. A Windows menu with highlighted commands.

Canceling Commands

If you choose the wrong command within a menu, you can select the Cancel button in that dialog box to cancel the command. This takes you back to the Main menu screen. If the command you choose opens a window without a cancel button, close the window by double-clicking on the Control-menu box (see Figure 2-1).

Command Extensions and Their Meanings

Some commands have an ellipsis (...) after them. When you select one of these commands, Windows displays a dialog box asking you to enter more information before the command is carried out. You learn more about dialog boxes in Lesson 4.

If a checkmark appears next to a command, the command is currently active within the program.

If you see a triangle next to the command, you have to choose an additional command in order to carry out the operation you want.

Working with the Control–Menu Box

The Control–menu box, as discussed in Lesson 2, is a small box in the upper left corner of the Program Manager window or other program windows. When you double-click on this box, the window is closed. When you click once on this box, the Control menu is displayed. This menu has a variety of commands that enable you to perform many operations (see Figure 3-3). The Control menu can also be displayed by pressing Alt+space bar.

The Control menu is accessible no matter where you are in Windows or what you are working on. The menu is available when you are in program windows, program icons, document windows, group icons, and dialog boxes.

Quitting Windows

In every instance, you quit Windows from the Program Manager after you have exited from any other Windows program you are using. Windows always gives you a chance to change your mind before the final exit to DOS.

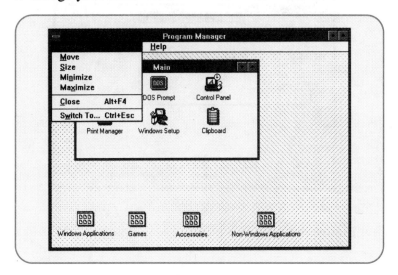

Figure 3-3. The Control menu.

If you are using a mouse:

1. Point to the File menu in the Program Manager and click the mouse button. The File menu will appear, as shown in Figure 3-4.

2. Point to the **Exit Windows** option and click the mouse button (see Figure 3-5). The End Session dialog box will appear.

3. If you made changes to Windows and want to save them, point to the Save Changes box and click. An X will appear in the box. Click again and the X will disappear.

4. If you want to exit Windows, point to the OK button and click. If you want to return to the Program Manager, point to the Cancel button and click.

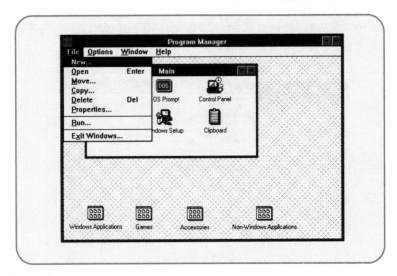

Figure 3-4. The File menu.

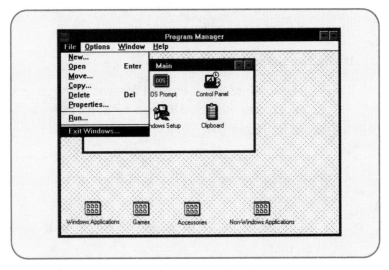

Figure 3-5. The Exit Windows option.

If you are using the keyboard:

1. Press Alt and then type F to open the File menu.

2. Type X to activate the Exit Windows dialog box. (Note that the X is underlined.)

3. If you want to save changes you made to Windows, press Tab until a dotted rectangle highlights the Save Changes box. Press the space bar to add an X to the Save Changes box. Press the space bar again and the X will disappear.

4. If you want to exit Windows, press Tab again to highlight the OK button and then press Enter. To return to the Program Manager, press Tab to highlight the Cancel button and then press Enter.

Exiting Windows from the Control Menu If you are using the mouse, double-click on the Control-menu box to go directly to the Exit Windows dialog box. If you are using the keyboard, go directly to the Exit Windows dialog box by pressing Alt-F4.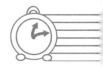

In this lesson, you learned about opening menus and selecting commands in Microsoft Windows. You also learned how to exit the program. In the next lesson, you'll learn more about finding your way around Windows by working with dialog boxes.

Working with Dialog Boxes

In this lesson, you'll learn how to open, use, and close dialog boxes.

What Is a Dialog Box?

Dialog boxes pop up on the screen after you select a certain command or begin a particular procedure. Dialog boxes request additional information, alert you if you have typed in something that doesn't allow Windows to run, and provide you with current data on the file you are using.

Boxes within Dialog Boxes

You may work with three different types of boxes within a Windows dialog box:

- Text boxes
- List boxes
- Drop-down list boxes

Working with Text Boxes

A text box is the area into which you type text information, such as a file name (see Figure 4-1). A text box may be empty, or it may already have text entered into it.

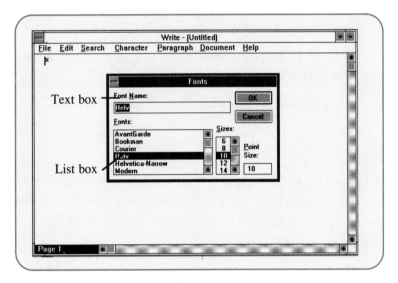

Figure 4-1. A command dialog box with options list.

If the text box is empty, enter your information by following these steps:

1. Place the cursor in the text box by clicking in the box with the mouse or by pressing Tab until the text box is highlighted.

2. Type the text, and then press Enter.

If the text box already has data in it, you may need to delete part or all of the information before you enter or edit your own. You can delete information several ways:

1. Place the cursor at the end of the text in the text box.

2. Press Del to erase all the text.

3. Type the new text.

   Or

1. Place the cursor anywhere within the text.

2. Press the Backspace or Delete key to remove the characters you want to delete.

3. Type the new text.

Working with List Boxes

A list box (refer to Figure 4-1) shows you a list of available options. The list box may also include scroll bars that enable you to move up and down in the list to choose the option that you need.

With most commands, list boxes let you choose options other than the default option that is selected automatically when the dialog box is opened. To select different options from a list box, use the following procedures.

If you are using a mouse:

1. Click on the arrows in the scroll bar to display selections above and below those shown in the list box.

2. Point to the selection you want and click. The selection you chose should replace the one that was in the text box. Then select the OK button.

If you are using the keyboard:

1. Press the Tab key to move the highlight to the list box you want.

2. Press the up- and down-arrow keys to move up and down the list until the selection you want is highlighted.

3. Press Enter.

What if the Dialog Box Doesn't Display a List?  If you open a dialog box and the pointer does not change into a cursor within the text box, the program is telling you that the entry in the box is the only one available for that command. In this case, make sure you are using the right command, or select OK and Windows will take you to the next screen.

In some list boxes, you can select more than one item. One example is a list box for a program that requires more than one file in order to run. To select more than one file from a list box, use the following procedures.

If you are using a mouse:

1. Point to each item you need, press Shift, and click the mouse button.

2. Select OK.

If you are using the keyboard:

1. Press the Tab key until the list box has the dotted rectangle around it.

2. Press the up- and down-arrow keys to highlight the first file you need.

3. Press the space bar to select the item. To cancel an item you've selected, highlight the item and press the space bar again.

27

4. Continue to use the arrow keys and the space bar until all the items you want are selected. Then press Enter.

Working with Drop-Down List Boxes

A drop-down list box is displayed as a separate box that has one item highlighted (the default option). Drop-down list boxes are used mainly in dialog boxes that don't have room for ordinary list boxes (see Figure 4-2).

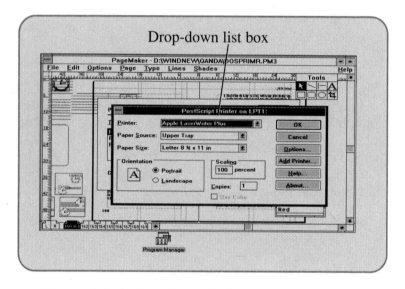

Figure 4-2. A drop-down list box.

To open and use a drop-down list box, follow the steps below.

If you are using a mouse:

1. Point to the boxed arrow at the right side of the drop-down list box and click the mouse button.

2. Click on the arrows in the scroll bar to scroll up and down through the list until your selection is visible.

3. Point to the selection you want and click. Then select OK.

If you are using the keyboard:

1. Press Alt+down arrow to open the drop-down list box.

2. Press the up- and down-arrow keys to scroll through the list until the item you need is highlighted.

3. Press Alt+up arrow or Alt+down arrow to select the highlighted option. (Press Esc to cancel box.) Then press Enter.

Selecting Options with Buttons and Boxes

Dialog boxes offer three other ways to select options (see Figure 4-3):

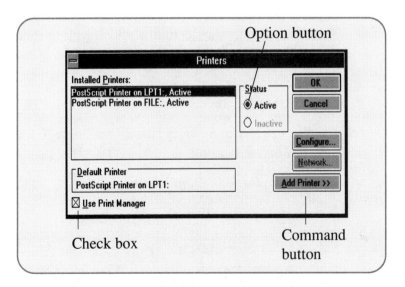

Figure 4-3. A dialog box with option buttons, command buttons, and check boxes.

- Option buttons

- Command buttons

- Check boxes

Option Buttons

Option buttons appear when you can select only one option in a group. You change options simply by choosing a different option button.

Notice in Figure 4-3 that an option is chosen when the button next to it is black. You cannot select an option if it is deselected (light gray). To select an option button in a dialog box, use the following procedures.

If you are using a mouse:

- Point to the button next to the option you want and click. The button should turn black. If you change your mind, click again and the button will be blank again.

If you are using the keyboard:

1. Use the Tab key to move the dotted rectangle to the group of option buttons.

2. Use the arrow keys to highlight the option you want.

3. Press Enter or select OK.

Selecting Option Buttons Quickly. If the option button you want includes an underlined letter, you can select the option button by holding down the Alt key and pressing the letter.

Command Buttons

Command buttons activate a final option that also closes the dialog box (refer to Figure 4-3). Commands such as Cancel, Continue, and OK appear as command buttons in most dialog boxes.

Command buttons with an ellipsis(...) after them take you to another dialog box where you need to supply more information.

Command options that are light gray are not available for the procedure you are using.

If a button is followed by two greater-than signs (>>), other options are available for that command (see Figure 4-4). Selecting the command shows you those other choices.

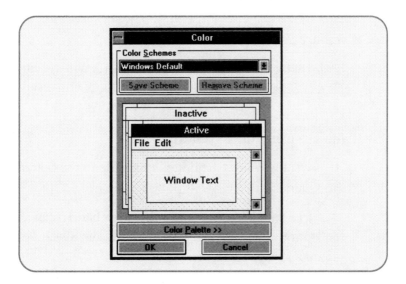

Figure 4-4. A command button with additional options.

Use the following procedures to choose a command within a dialog box.

If you are using a mouse:

- Point to the command you want and click.

If you are using the keyboard:

- Press Tab until the command you need is surrounded by the dotted rectangle, and then press Enter or the space bar.

Check Boxes

Check boxes are used to turn options on and off within a dialog box (refer to Figure 4-3). You can select as many check boxes in a Window as you need. When a check box has been chosen, an X appears in the box. If an item is light gray, it is not available for selection. To choose a check box, use the following procedures.

If you are using a mouse:

- Point to the box you want and click. An X will appear. To cancel a selection, click again and the X will disappear.

If you are using the keyboard:

1. Press Tab to move the dotted rectangle to the option you want.

2. To place an X in the box, press the space bar. To cancel an option that you don't want, press the space bar again and the X will disappear.

Closing Dialog Boxes

To close a dialog box that is displayed on-screen and discontinue a procedure, select the **Cancel** option. You can also close a dialog box in three other ways:

- Click on or select the Control-menu box and choose the **Close** option.

- Press the Esc key on the keyboard.

- Select OK to close the dialog box and continue with a procedure.

In this lesson, you learned what dialog boxes are and how to use them. In the next lesson, you'll learn how to start and quit programs within Windows.

Lesson 5

Starting and Quitting Programs within Windows

In this lesson, you'll learn how to start and quit programs within Windows.

Starting Programs

In Windows, there are three ways to start a program:

- From the Program Manager by using a group window or an icon

- From the File Manager by choosing program files from a list

- From the File or Program Manager by choosing the **Run** command

The Program Manager enables you to create icons for specific programs so that you can open the program from within a group window. This particular method of using programs within Windows is popular because of its convenience. Within the Program Manager, you can start a program by using a mouse or the keyboard.

The Program Manager is the easiest way to run programs that have been set up in Windows with specific icons. You can use either the File Manager or the **Run** command to run programs that are *not* set up as icons. Use the File Manager if you are not sure of the program file name. If you know the file name, you can use **Run** to shortcut the procedure.

Using the Program Manager

To start a program in the Program Manager, use the following procedures.

If you are using a mouse:

1. At the Main menu screen, the Program Manager and its group windows should be visible (see Figure 5-1). Point to the program icon that contains the file you want and double-click. Another screen will appear showing the directories that are available within that program icon.

2. Point to the directory name and double-click. The files within that directory will appear.

3. Point to the file name and double-click.

If you are using the keyboard:

1. Return to the Program Manager window and Main menu screen.

2. Using the arrow keys, highlight the program icon you want, and then press Enter. You should see a screen showing more icons (see Figure 5-2).

3. Using the arrow keys, highlight the icon you want, and then press Enter.

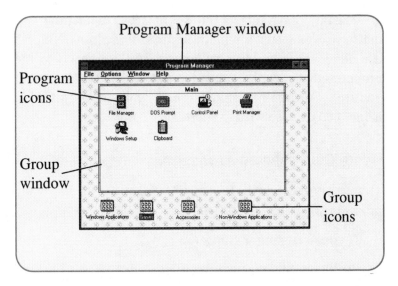

Figure 5-1. The Program Manager with group window icons.

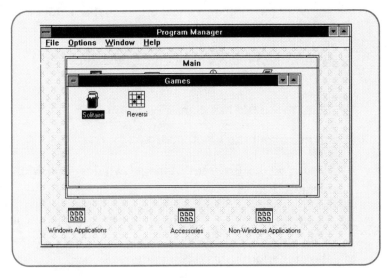

Figure 5-2. Group window icons.

Using the File Manager

To start a program in the File Manager, use the following procedures.

If you are using a mouse:

1. Point to the File Manager icon and double-click. You should see the directory tree.

2. Point to the directory containing the program you want and double-click. The files in the directory you chose will be displayed (see Figure 5-3).

3. Point to the file you want and double-click. The file you need should now appear.

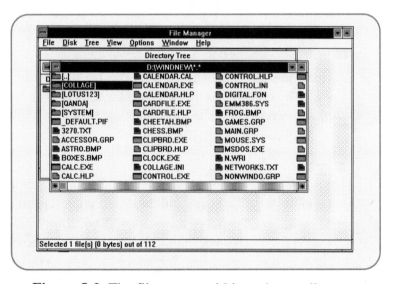

Figure 5-3. The file screen within a chosen directory.

If you are using the keyboard:

1. Return to the Main menu screen; the File Manager icon should appear in the window.

37

2. Use the arrow keys to highlight the File Manager icon, and then press Enter. You should now be at the directory tree.

3. Use the up- and down-arrow keys until the directory that you want is highlighted, and then press Enter. The directory you chose will be displayed (refer to Figure 5-3).

4. Use the arrow keys to highlight the file you want and press Enter.

Using the Run Command

To start a program using the **Run** command, follow these steps:

1. Go to the Main menu screen in the Program Manager window.

2. Open the File menu and select the **Run** command either by pointing to the command and double-clicking or by typing **R**. The Run command dialog box will be displayed with a flashing cursor in the text box (see Figure 5-4).

3. To open the file you want, type the drive name (usually **A**, **B**, **C**, or **D**), followed by a colon(:) and a backslash(\). Then type the name of the directory, followed by another backslash. Type the exact name of the file you want to open, and select OK or press Enter.

Quitting Programs

Within Windows there are three ways to quit a program that is running:

- From the File menu in the Program Manager window, by clicking the mouse button on the **Exit** option or by typing **X** on the keyboard

- From the Control menu, by clicking the mouse button on the **Close** option or by typing **C** on the keyboard

- By double-clicking on the Control-menu box

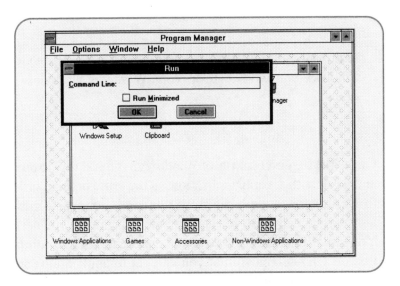

Figure 5-4. The Run command dialog box.

The file will close and take you back to the Main menu screen with the Program Manager window.

By now you should be able to start and quit programs within Windows 3. In this lesson, you learned how to start programs using the Program Manager, the File Manager, and the **Run** command. You also learned that you can quit programs using three simple methods, regardless of the program you are using. In the next lesson, you'll learn how to move individual windows displayed in the Windows desktop. Later lessons explain the Program Manager, File Manager, and the directory tree in more detail.

Moving
Windows

In this lesson, you'll learn how to move and resize the windows you work with in your Windows work sessions.

One of the biggest benefits of Windows 3 is the ability to open and work with several applications at the same time. In order to use the applications efficiently, you need to be able to move and rearrange them so you can find the information you need. You move and resize windows to help organize the information on your screen so that you can get to applications and documents efficiently.

Getting Ready To Move Windows

The way you move windows depends on the type of window you are using and whether you are using the mouse or the keyboard.

The two types of windows you work with are application windows and document windows.

- *Application windows* are screens that contain running programs, such as Windows Write or Microsoft Word for Windows. The name of the application will appear at the top of the window when you are using it.

- *Document windows* appear inside application windows and contain documents or files. These screens have a title bar with menu options.

When you use the mouse to move a window, the mouse pointer changes to one of four different shapes, depending on the operation. These pointers and their descriptions are introduced in Table 6-1.

Table 6-1. Pointer Shape for Moving Windows

Pointer	Description
↖	Moves the window to a different place on the screen.
↖	Moves the corner of the window in any direction.
↕	Moves the edge of the window up or down.
↔	Moves the edge of the window to the left or right.

When you use the keyboard to move or resize a window, you use the options in the Control menu (see Figure 6-1). To open the Control menu, press Alt+space bar.

Opening the Control Menu from within a Document If you need to open the Control menu when you are working in an application, press Alt+hyphen.\

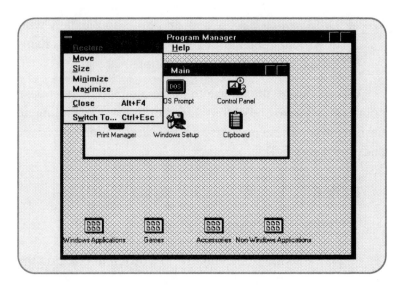

Figure 6-1. The Control menu.

When you are using the keyboard and Control menu to move windows, you use the commands listed in Table 6-2.

Table 6-2. Commands Used To Move Windows

Command	Description	Shortcut Key
	Select Window	Alt+Esc Ctrl+F6
Restore	Returns a window to its original size (available only if the window has previously been resized)	Alt+F5 (application) Ctrl+F5 (document)
Move	Enables you to move the selected window	Alt+F7 (application) Ctrl+F7 (document)
Size	Enables you to change the size of a window by moving its edge	Alt+F8 (application) Ctrl+F8 (document)

Table 6-2. (continued)

Command	Description	Shortcut Key
Minimize	Changes the window to an icon	Alt+F9 (application)
Maximize	Enlarges the size of a screen to its maximum	Alt+F10 (application) Ctrl+F10 (document)

Moving Windows and Icons

To move a window using a mouse,

1. Place the pointer in the title bar of the window.

2. Press and hold the mouse button.

3. Move the mouse in the direction you want to move the window.

   When you move the mouse, an outline of the window will follow the pointer (see Figure 6-2).

4. When the window is positioned where you want it, release the mouse button.

Canceling Operations To cancel the procedure, press Esc before you release the mouse button.

To move a window using the keyboard:

1. Choose the window you want to move by pressing Alt-Esc (in an application window) or Ctrl+F6 (in a document window). The highlight moves from window to window (see Figure 6-3).

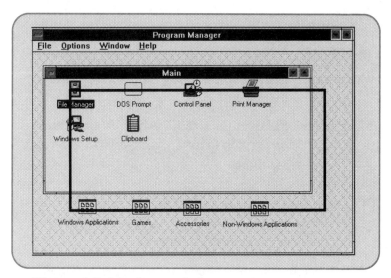

Figure 6-2. Moving a window.

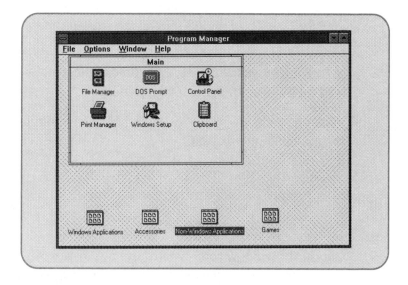

Figure 6-3. Selecting a window.

2. Select the window you want to move.

3. Open the Control menu.

4. Press **M** to select the **Move** command. The cursor changes to a four-sided arrow.

5. Use the arrow keys to move the window.

6. When the window is positioned where you want it, press Enter.

In this lesson, you learned how to move the windows on your screen. In the next lesson you'll learn how to resize windows.

Resizing Windows

In this lesson, you'll learn how to resize the windows in the Windows desktop.

Changing the Size of a Window

You have several options for changing the size of a window. You can

- Resize a window to make more room for the display of other windows

- Shrink an application to an icon to give you more space on-screen

- Enlarge a window to its maximum size

- Restore a window to its original size

To change the size of a window using a mouse, follow these steps:

1. Place the pointer on the corner of the window you would like to resize. The pointer should change to a double arrow.

2. Hold the mouse button and drag the corner until the window is the size you would like it to be.

3. Release the mouse button.

Changing the Height or Width of a Window

You may want to change only the height or width of a window rather than the total size. To shorten or lengthen a window, position the pointer on the bottom border of the window before pressing the mouse button. To change only the width, position the pointer on the edge of the window you want to move. Notice that the pointer changes to a double arrow. Then hold the mouse button and drag the edge of the window to the desired size.

To resize the window using the keyboard:

1. Select the window to resize.

2. Select the window you want from the displayed list.

3. Open the Control menu.

4. Press S to choose the Size command.

5. Use the arrow keys to move the pointer to the border or corner you want to move.

6. When the pointer is positioned on the border or corner, use the arrow keys to resize the screen. Notice that an outline of the window will follow the arrow as you make changes.

7. When the window is the size you want, press Enter.

Shrinking a Window to an Icon

Windows gives you the option of shrinking a window to an icon. This gives you maximum space available on-screen, while allowing you to reopen and work with the window easily.

To shrink a window to an icon using a mouse, follow these steps:

1. Select the window you would like to reduce to an icon.

2. Place the pointer on the Minimize button on-screen and click the mouse button (see Figure 7-1).

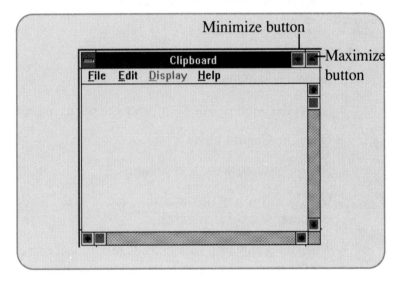

Figure 7-1. The Minimize and Maximize buttons.

To shrink a window using the keyboard:

1. Select the window you want to shrink.

2. Open the Control menu.

3. Press N to choose the Minimize command.

Enlarging a Window

If you are working on a single document, it may be helpful to have that document fill the entire screen, especially if the document has figures and graphics.

To enlarge a window using a mouse, follow these steps:

1. Choose the window you want to enlarge.

2. Click the Maximize button.

To enlarge a window using the keyboard, follow these steps:

1. Select the window to enlarge.

2. Open the Control menu.

3. Press X to choose the Maximize command.

Restoring a Window

Restoring applies to windows that have been enlarged to full size or reduced to icons. Restoring a window changes it back to the size it was before you enlarged or reduced it.

To restore an icon back to a window, follow these steps.

If you are using a mouse:

1. Place the pointer on the icon you want to restore.

2. Double-click the mouse button.

If you are using the keyboard:

1. Select the icon you want to restore.

2. Open the Control menu.

3. Press R to choose the Restore command.

49

To change an enlarged window back to its original size, follow these steps.

If you are using a mouse:

1. Place the pointer on the **Restore** command shown in Figure 7-2.

2. Click the mouse button.

If you are using the keyboard:

1. Open the Control menu.

2. Press **R** to choose the **Restore** command.

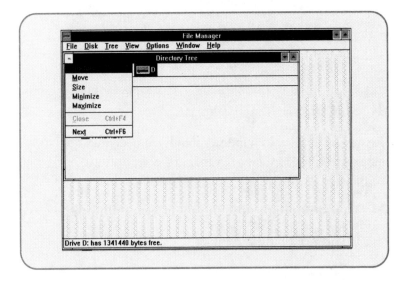

Figure 7-2. Restoring a window.

In this lesson, you learned to resize windows, shrink them into icons, and enlarge them to full screen size. You also learned to return an icon or enlarged window to its original size. In the next lesson you'll learn how to work with more than one window at the same time.

Lesson 8

Working with Multiple Windows

In this lesson, you'll learn about working with and switching between multiple windows.

Using Multiple Windows

One of the most powerful features in Windows 3 is the ability to work with two or more applications at the same time. This feature not only saves time but allows you to work efficiently. For example, you might work with a word processor and a desktop publishing program simultaneously, inputting information into a word processor, and then transferring it into a formal desktop published document with headings, text sizes, and spacing already set.

Switching between Windows Applications

When you are working with multiple windows, you need to be able to switch between them. This can be done two ways:

- Switching between visible windows on-screen

Or

- Switching between windows from the Task list

Switching between Visible Windows On-Screen

The most common way to work in Windows 3 is to run one window application at a time, with other available applications shown as icons.

These icons give you easy accessibility to a variety of applications. If you are working in a window and need to open another application from an icon, follow these steps.

If you are using a mouse:

1. Place the pointer on the application icon you want to open.

2. Double-click the mouse button.

If you are using the keyboard:

1. Press Ctrl-Tab until the application icon you need is highlighted.

2. Press Enter.

After you switch into the new application, the window you were working with changes to an icon.

Working with the Task List

Switching between visible windows works best when you are working with applications one at a time. However, you may need to use more than one running application at a time.

The Task list lets you move among different applications that are running at the same time (see Figure 8-1). It allows you to cascade and tile windows so that you can work with multiple windows. To move from one running application to another, follow these steps.

If you are using a mouse:

1. Double-click the mouse button on any part of the desktop or select the Switch To option in the Control menu. The Task list window appears.

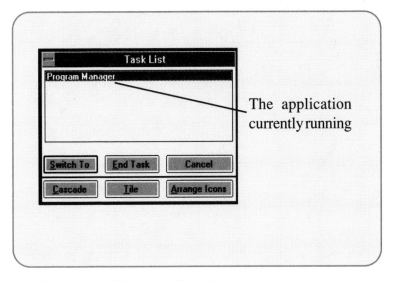

The application currently running

Figure 8-1. The Task list window.

2. Place the pointer on the window you want to open.

3. Click the mouse button.

4. Place the pointer on the Switch To option.

5. Click the mouse button.

If you are using the keyboard:

1. Press Ctrl+Esc to display the Task list window.

2. Use the arrow keys to highlight the application you want to open.

3. Press Enter.

In this lesson, you learned to use multiple windows. In the next lesson you'll learn how to copy, cut, and paste data from one application window to another.

Lesson 9

Copying, Cutting, and Pasting between Applications

In this lesson, you'll learn how to transfer data among Windows applications.

Within the many applications that you use, copying, cutting, and pasting information will be vital. When you cut information, you are removing it from its current location in Windows. Copying data makes a duplicate of the information you need while leaving the original data in its place. Pasting data is placing cut or copied information into a new location in an application.

Understanding the Clipboard

When you cut or copy data, Windows places the information on an unseen clipboard. When you paste the information into a document, Windows copies the data from the clipboard and places it at the point you specify. The clipboard holds only one piece of information at a time, so each time you cut or copy data, Windows replaces the last item on the clipboard with the new information.

You can display the information currently on the clipboard by following these steps.

1. Go to the Main menu screen.

2. Use the pointer or the arrow keys to highlight the clip-board icon.

3. Double-click the mouse button or press Enter. The clipboard is then displayed (see Figure 9-1).

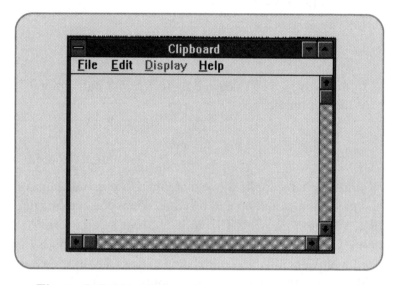

Figure 9-1. The clipboard.

Copying or Cutting Information

Copying or cutting data enables you to transfer information from one application to another. You can copy or cut as little as one word and as much as an entire screen. You can also copy information from a non-Windows application.

To copy or cut data from an application in Windows, follow these steps.

If you are using a mouse:

1. Click the mouse button to the left of the data you want

to cut or copy and hold the button. The pointer will change to an I-beam cursor.

2. Drag the cursor across the information until the data you need is highlighted.

3. Release the mouse button.

Removing the Highlight If you want to change the highlighted information or find that you've made a mistake, click the mouse button anywhere on the screen and the highlight will disappear.

4. Open the Edit menu.

5. Select the **Copy** or **Cut** command.

6. Click the mouse button and the information will be placed on the clipboard.

If you are using the keyboard:

1. Use the arrow keys to move the cursor just before the text you want to cut or copy.

2. Highlight the data by pressing the Shift key and the appropriate arrow key until the data you need is highlighted.

3. Release the keys.

4. Press Alt+E to activate the Edit menu.

5. Use the arrow keys to highlight the **Cut** or **Copy** command.

6. Press Enter, and the information is placed on the clipboard.

Copying a Full Screen

To copy an entire screen, follow these steps:

1. Display the screen you want to copy.

2. Press the Print Screen key, and the information is copied to the clipboard.

When you press Print Screen, the computer takes a picture of the screen and places it on the clipboard. If for some reason the Print Screen option does not work, you have two alternatives:

● Press Alt+Print Screen.

Or

● Press Shift+Print Screen.

Pasting Information in Windows

After you copy or cut information, you may want to place it somewhere. The Paste command allows you to place data into another application in the exact form in which it was copied or cut. Most applications recognize both text and graphics when pasting.

To paste information into an application, follow these steps:

1. Make sure the information you want to paste is on the clipboard.

2. Open the document or application into which you want to paste the information.

3. Use the pointer or the arrow keys to place the cursor where you want the data to be pasted.

4. Point to Edit and click the mouse button, or press Alt+E.

5. Select the Paste option.

In this lesson, you learned to copy, cut, and paste information in different windows. In the next lesson, you'll explore the capabilities of the Program Manager.

Introducing the Program Manager

In this lesson, you'll learn about group windows, group icons, and program icons.

Understanding the Program Manager

The Program Manager is the central nervous system of Windows 3. As soon as you start Windows 3, the Program Manager is activated and continues to run as long as you remain in Windows.

The Program Manager ties together applications and documents within Windows 3. It also enables you to open and work with application and document windows by simply double-clicking on the appropriate icon. The Program Manager screen is shown in Figure 10-1.

There are three main sections within the Program Manager:

- Group Windows
- Group Icons
- Program Icons

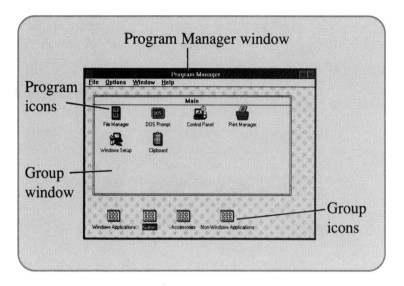

Figure 10-1. The Program Manager window.

Group Windows and Group Icons

Group windows are windows from which you can load applications or documents that run within Windows. Similar applications and documents are grouped together so that you can find them easily. For example, the Games group window supplied with Windows contains games such as Solitaire and Reversi.

Group windows are represented on the Program Manager window by group icons, located in the lower part of the screen in Figure 10-1. You use group icons to open group windows.

Try the following example. At the bottom of the Program Manager screen is a group icon with the name Games. To open this group window,

1. Point to or highlight the Games icon.

2. Double-click the mouse button or press Enter.

The Games group window opens, displaying the applications within the group (see Figure 10-2). When you create your own group windows in the next lesson, you will follow this organization by placing similar or related programs or files in a group.

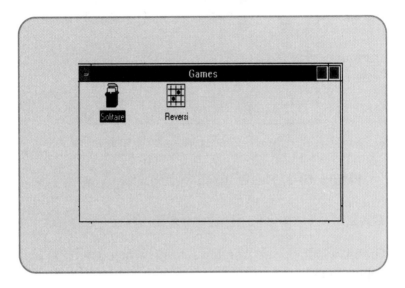

Figure 10-2. The icons in the Games group window.

 Closing the Control menu You can double-click on the Control menu to close a group window and reduce it to an icon.

When you're finished using a particular application or document, you need to reduce the group window to its original icon size.

To reduce a group window to an icon, follow these steps:

1. Open the Control menu.

2. Choose the Minimize option if you plan to return to the application again in this work session, or select

Close if you are finished working with the application.

Minimizing Windows You can quickly reduce a window to an icon by clicking on the minimize button (shown as a down-arrow symbol) on the right side of the top border of the screen.

Program Icons

A program icon represents a particular application or document in a group window. To activate a program icon, such as Solitaire in the Games group window, follow these steps:

1. Open the group window that contains the application you want to run (in this case, Games).

2. Point to or highlight the program icon you want.

3. Double-click the mouse button or press Enter.

You can change an open window into a program icon if you need workspace as discussed in Lesson 7.

Group Windows Included with Windows 3

Windows 3 automatically created a few group windows for you:

● The Main group window

● The Accessories window

● The Games window

The Main Group Window

The Main group window appears as soon as you start the program from the Program Manager. The Main group window contains many of the programs that make Windows as powerful as it is:

- File Manager

- DOS Prompt

- Control Panel

- Print Manager

- Windows Setup

- Clipboard

Figure 10-3 shows an example of the Main group window.

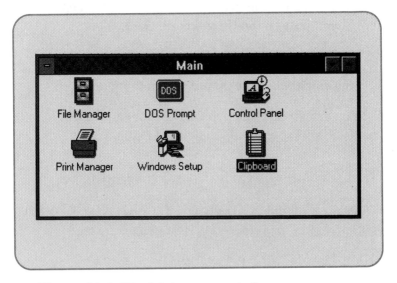

Figure 10-3. The Main group window.

The Accessories and Games Group Windows

The Accessories window provides you with desktop functions that make working in Windows 3 easier. Some of these accessories include a calculator, calendar, and a word processing program. Other applications in this window include a paintbrush program, a card file to organize phone numbers and addresses, and a clock. Additionally, the games in the Games Window can give you a break from the traditional tasks you perform in Windows 3.

In this lesson, you worked with group windows, group icons, and program icons. In the next lesson you'll learn how to create group windows.

Creating Group Windows

In this lesson, you'll learn how to create your own group windows.

Creating a New Group Window

Although the group windows included within Windows are a start, you'll want to create your own groups as you begin working with Windows 3.

To create a group window, follow these steps:

1. Open the File menu in the Program Manager window.

2. Choose the New option.

3. Select the Program Group option.

4. Click on OK or press Enter. The Program Group Properties dialog box is then displayed.

5. Type a description of the window you want to create (this assigns a title to the new group window).

6. Click on OK or press Enter.

Adding Program Icons to a New Group Window

Once you've created the group window, you can add program icons. You do this in one of three ways:

- Using the New option from the File menu in the Program Manager

- Using the Windows Setup option in the Main menu

- Using application and document files from the File Manager

Because this lesson focuses on the Program Manager, we'll explain only the first method. For more information on adding program icons using the other techniques, consult your documentation or a book on Windows, such as *The First Book of Microsoft Windows 3.0.*

To add a program icon to a newly created group window from within the Program Manager, follow these steps:

1. Open your new Group window.

2. Open the Program Manager's File menu.

3. Select the New option. The Program Item Properties dialog box appears on-screen.

4. Choose the Program Item option and select OK.

5. In the description box, type a description of the program icon you are adding. This assigns a name to the icon.

6. Move the cursor to the Command Line box.

7. Type the program file name (remember to include the file's extension).

Determining the Program Name If you don't know the program name or extension, select the Browse button and you will be shown a list of files and extensions to choose from.

8. If you are adding a document, add a space and type the file name of the document.

9. Click on OK or press Enter.

Windows then adds the new program icon to your group window.

Arranging Group Windows

You can arrange your group windows by manually moving or resizing them, as described in Lessons 6 and 7.

You can also have the Program Manager arrange windows for you in two different ways:

● Cascading windows

● Tiling windows

Cascading Windows

When the Program Manager cascades windows for you, it changes the size of the group windows and stacks them one over the other so that only the title in each appears. An example of cascading group windows is shown in Figure 11-1.

To cascade windows, follow these steps:

1. Open the Window menu from the Program Manager screen.

2. Choose the Cascade option.

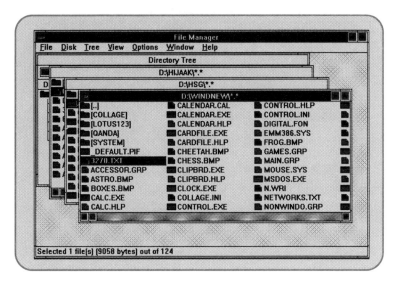

File Manager

| File | Disk | Tree | View | Options | Window | Help |

Directory Tree

D:\HIJAAK*.*

D:\HSG*.*

D:\WINDNEW*.*

[..]	CALENDAR.CAL	CONTROL.HLP
[COLLAGE]	CALENDAR.EXE	CONTROL.INI
[LOTUS123]	CALENDAR.HLP	DIGITAL.FON
[QANDA]	CARDFILE.EXE	EMM386.SYS
[SYSTEM]	CARDFILE.HLP	FROG.BMP
DEFAULT.PIF	CHEETAH.BMP	GAMES.GRP
3270.TXT	CHESS.BMP	MAIN.GRP
ACCESSOR.GRP	CLIPBRD.EXE	MOUSE.SYS
ASTRO.BMP	CLIPBRD.HLP	MSDOS.EXE
BOXES.BMP	CLOCK.EXE	N.WRI
CALC.EXE	COLLAGE.INI	NETWORKS.TXT
CALC.HLP	CONTROL.EXE	NONWINDO.GRP

Selected 1 file[s] [9058 bytes] out of 124

Figure 11-1. Cascading group windows.

Cascading Windows From the keyboard, you can press Shift+F5 to activate the **Cascade** option.

Tiling Windows

Tiling separates the screen into different areas, each of which contains a group window as shown in Figure 11-2. This method of arranging windows is helpful when you are working with a large number of program icons in different groups.

To tile group windows, follow these steps:

1. Open the Window menu from the Program Manager screen.

2. Choose the Tile option.

Tiling Windows From the keyboard, you can tile windows quickly by pressing Shift+F4.

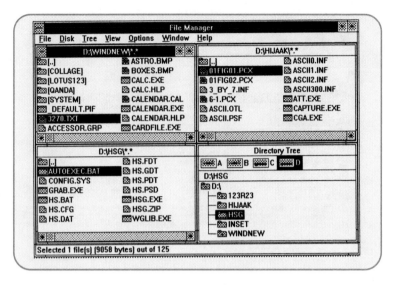

Figure 11-2. Tiled group windows.

Arranging Icons within Windows

You can also have Windows rearrange the icons within windows. To do this, follow these steps:

1. Open the Window menu.

2. Select the Arrange Icons option.

Windows then aligns the icons in the windows.

Deleting Groups

As your work with Windows progresses, there will be times when you no longer need a particular group window. Once you're finished with a group, you can delete it from the Program Manager.

Note: Deleting the group window does not erase the program or data files you have included in that group.

To delete a group window, follow these steps:

1. Minimize the group window to icon size.

2. Point to or highlight the group icon.

3. Open the File menu.

4. Select the Delete option. A warning box appears, telling you that an icon is about to be deleted.

5. Choose Yes or type Y.

In this lesson, you learned about creating group windows within the Program Manager. The next lesson introduces you to the File Manager.

Introducing the File Manager

In this lesson, you'll learn how to find your way around directories using the File Manager and the directory tree.

Starting the File Manager

The File Manager enables you to organize your files and directories, so you can find what you need easily. To start the File Manager, follow these steps:

1. From the Program Manager, point to or highlight the File Manager icon.

2. Double-click the mouse button or press Enter.

The first screen of the File Manager, known as the *directory tree*, appears (see Figure 12-1).

Using the Directory Tree

The directory tree displays important information about the directory you are working in. For example, in Figure 12-1, the various available disk drives are represented as icons, and the currently selected disk drive is highlighted. Just below the disk drive icons the directory path is displayed. In the main area of the screen a tree structure displays all the files in the current directory.

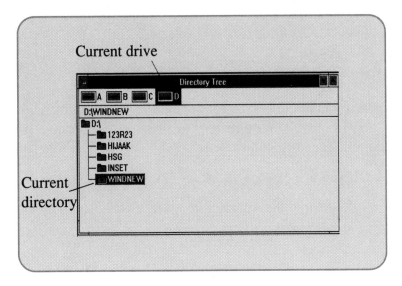

Figure 12-1. The directory tree.

You use the directory tree to do the following things:

- Display the contents of a different disk drive

- Change directories

- Open directory windows

Changing Drives

To display the contents of a disk drive other than the currently selected drive. Use the following steps:

1. Point to the drive icons, or press the arrow keys until the highlight moves to the drive icons line.

2. Click on the drive you want to display, or press the arrow keys until the drive is highlighted and then press Enter.

A new directory tree is then displayed, showing the contents of the drive you have selected.

Changing Directories

When you are using the File Manager, you will invariably want to move from directory to directory. To change the current directory, follow these steps.

If you are using a mouse:

1. Point to the directory you want.

2. Click the mouse button.

If you are using the keyboard, use the keys in Table 12-1 to move the highlight to the directory you want.

Table 12-1. Keys for Moving to Directories

Key	Moves the Highlight to
Up arrow	Directory above current one
Down arrow	Directory below current one
Right arrow	Subdirectory of current directory
Left arrow	Next highest level of current directory
Ctrl+Up arrow	Previous directory at same level
Ctrl+Down arrow	Next directory at same level
Home	Root directory

Finding a Directory Quickly If you know the name of the directory you want, you can quickly make that directory the current one by typing the first letter of the directory name. The highlight then moves to the directory that matches the letter you typed.

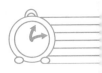

Try using the keyboard method.

1. Press the down-arrow key.

2. Press Ctrl+up arrow.

3. Press Home. The highlight should now be at the top of the directory tree, with the root directory as the current directory. (*Note*: For more information about directories, see the "DOS Primer" at the back of this book.)

Using Directory Windows

After you've found the drive and directory you need, you're ready to open a directory window and look at some files. In directory windows, you can

- Display contents of directories

- Display file information

- Sort and redisplay the files

Opening a Directory Window

To open a directory window, follow these steps:

1. From the directory tree, point to or highlight the directory you want to view.

2. Double-click the mouse button or press Enter.

Windows then displays the current directory in a window on-screen (see Figure 12-2).

At the top of the directory window, you see the disk drive and path of the current directory. At the far right, you see Minimize and Maximize buttons. On the far left, the Control-menu box appears. In the main area of the screen, you see a list of files in the current directory.

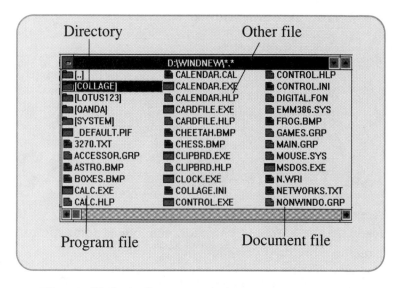

Figure 12-2. A directory window.

Depending on the types of files and directories in the window, you may see several different icons. Directories are displayed as file folders; program files appear as envelopes; document files look like the page of a notepad; all other files have icons resembling a blank notepad page.

 Arranging Directory Windows You can have Windows arrange the current directory window for you by choosing **Cascade** or **Tile** from the Window menu.

Closing Directory Windows

Although you can have several directory windows open at once, only one can be active. To close the current directory window, follow these steps.

If you are using a mouse:

1. Position the mouse pointer on the Control-menu box.

2. Double-click the mouse button.

If you are using the keyboard:

1. Press Alt+hyphen (-) to display the Control menu.

2. Use the arrow keys to highlight Close.

3. Press Enter.

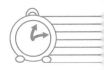

Closing All Directory Windows You can close all open directory windows by opening the Window menu and choosing the **Close All Directories** option.

In this lesson we introduced the File Manager and how it works in Windows. In the next lesson you'll learn how to use directories.

Working with Directories

In this lesson, you'll learn how to set up and use directories.

Creating and Using Directories

Although the File Manager displays the files and directories already set up within Windows, you will want to create and organize directories containing your own files. This section explains how to create directories and work with files and directories.

Creating Directories

To create a directory, follow these steps:

1. From the directory tree, highlight the directory in which you want to create the new directory. (*Note*: The new directory will be a subdirectory of the current directory. If you want to create a new directory that is not a subdirectory of an existing directory, highlight the root directory.)

2. Open the File menu.

3. Select the Create Directory option.

4. Type a name for the directory.

5. Click on OK or press Enter.

Copying Files and Directories

You can copy a directory or files one of two ways, depending on whether you are using the mouse or the keyboard.

If you are using a mouse:

1. Press the Ctrl key and drag the directory (or files) you want to copy over to the drive, window, or icon where you want to store the copy.

2. Release the mouse button.

3. Release the Ctrl key. You are asked to confirm the copy.

4. Click on Yes.

If you are using the keyboard:

1. Highlight the directory (or file) you want to copy.

2. Open the File menu.

3. Choose the Copy option.

4. Type the path to the drive, window, or icon in which you want to store the copy.

5. Press C to choose Copy.

Moving Files and Directories

Occasionally, you'll want to reorganize the files on your system. This may include moving files and directories. You can move files and directories by following these steps.

If you are using a mouse:

1. Press the Alt key and drag the directory (or file) you want to move over to the drive, window, or icon where you want to move the directory (or file).

2. Release the mouse button.

3. Release the Alt key. You are asked to confirm the move.

4. Click on Yes.

If you are using the keyboard:

1. Highlight the directory (or file) you want to move.

2. Open the File menu.

3. Choose the Move option.

4. Type the path to the drive, window, or icon where you want to move the directory (or file).

5. Press Enter.

Renaming Files and Directories

You can also rename files and directories from within the File Manager. To rename files and directories, follow these steps:

1. Select the directory or file you want to rename.

2. Open the File menu.

3. Choose the Rename option.

4. Type the new name for the file in the To box.

5. Click on Rename or type R.

Deleting Files and Directories

The File Manager lets you delete unwanted files and directories easily. Be careful when you are planning to delete anything—especially directories that contain files—from your system. Once a file is deleted, it's gone, unless you have a recovery program that will help you retrieve accidentally deleted files.

To delete files and directories, follow these steps:

1. Highlight the directory (or file) you want to delete.

2. Open the File menu.

3. Choose Delete. You are asked to confirm that you want to delete the selected file or directory.

4. Select Yes to carry out the deletion.

Exiting the File Manager

When you're ready to exit the File Manager, follow these steps:

1. Open the File menu.

2. Click on Exit or type X.

3. Make sure an X is displayed in the Save Settings box (if not, press Tab to get to the box and press the space bar or click on the box).

4. Click on OK or press Enter.

In this lesson, you learned the basics of working with directories using the File Manager. The next lesson enables you to customize your Windows work session by using the Control Panel.

Introducing the Control Panel

In this lesson, you will learn how to work with the Control Panel in Windows 3.

Operating the Control Panel

The Control Panel gives you the ability to customize Windows 3. The Control Panel is shown as a group icon on the Main menu screen in the Program Manager window (see Figure 14-1). The Control Panel enables you to perform the following operations:

- Change color schemes on-screen

- Add or delete fonts

- Alter the speed of your mouse

- Move and resize objects on your desktop

- Connect ports for quicker system manipulations

- Install printers

- Change international options which include: language, date, time, and currency

- Alter the keyboard repeat rate

- Reset the date and time on your system

- Turn the warning beep in Windows 3 on or off

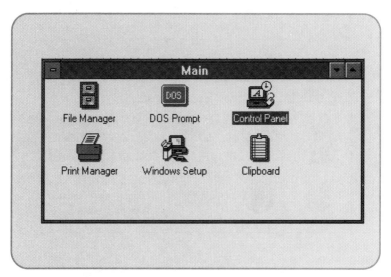

Figure 14-1. The Control Panel icon.

Opening the Control Panel

To open the Control Panel, follow these steps:

1. Open the Main window.

2. Move the mouse pointer or highlight the Control Panel icon.

3. Double-click the mouse button or press Enter.

The Control Panel is displayed with a group of icons that enable you to customize various elements in your system (see Figure 14-2).

To select one of the Control Panel options, follow these steps:

1. Point to or highlight the icon of the option you want.

2. Double-click the mouse button or press Enter.

Figure 14-2. The Control Panel window.

The Settings and Help Menus

The Settings and Help menus are available to you after the Control Panel has been activated. You can find both of these menus in the top left corner of the Control Panel window.

The Settings Menu

The Settings menu is an alternative way of opening the icons in the Control Panel. You can also find the command which allows you to exit the Control Panel here. To open the Settings menu, follow these steps:

1. Point to the word Settings.

2. Click the mouse button.

Or

● Press Alt-S on the keyboard.

You will see a list of options identical to the icons in the Control Panel window. To select an option,

1. Point to or highlight the option you want.

2. Click the mouse button or press Enter.

The Help Menu

The Help menu assists you if you are having trouble understanding the Control Panel options. Some of the help options include the following:

● Working with the Control Panel index

● Using the keyboard

● Choosing commands in the Control Panel

● Working with procedures

● How to use the Help menu

● A basic overview of the Control Panel

To activate the Help menu, follow these steps:

1. Point to the word Help.

2. Click the mouse button.

Or

● Press Alt-H.

To select a help option from the list that is displayed, follow these steps:

1. Point to or highlight the desired option.

2. Click the mouse button or press Enter.

Exiting the Control Panel

To exit the Control Panel, follow these steps.

If you are using a mouse:

1. Open the Settings menu.

2. Click on the Exit option.

If you are using the keyboard:

1. Press Alt-S.

2. Press X.

In this lesson, you learned how to open, work with, and exit the Control Panel. In the next lesson you'll learn how to further customize Windows.

Lesson 15

Working with Color Schemes in the Control Panel

In this lesson, you'll learn how to choose the colors displayed on your Windows screen.

The color application in the Control Panel enables you to change the color of the screens you are working with, by

- Choosing from existing color schemes within Windows 3

- Creating your own color scheme

Choosing an Existing Color Scheme

After you select the Color icon, you click on the down arrow in the Color Schemes box to see a dialog box that lists all the color schemes available within Windows 3 (see Figure 15-1). To choose one of the displayed color schemes, follow these steps.

If you are using a mouse:

1. Click on the scroll arrow in the Color list dialog box until the color you want appears.

2. Click on OK.

87

If you are using the keyboard:

1. Press Tab until the Color list box is highlighted.

2. Press the down-arrow key until the color you want is shown.

3. Press Enter.

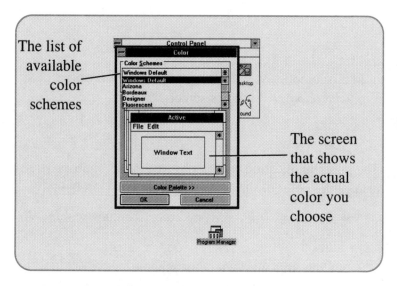

Figure 15-1. The Color application window.

Creating a New Color Scheme

To create a different color scheme from those displayed in the color list, follow these steps:

1. Select the Color option in the Control Panel.

2. Point to or highlight Color Palette.

3. Click the mouse button or press Enter.

A window displays the screen elements and shows you the variety of colors available (see Figure 15-2).

To create a new color scheme, follow these steps:

1. Scroll through the list of elements until the one you need is highlighted.

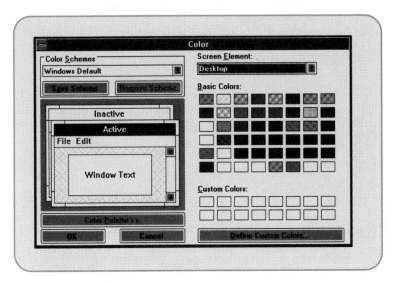

Figure 15-2. Selecting screen colors.

2. Click the mouse button on the color you would like the selected element to be, or, use the arrow keys to highlight the color.

3. To save your changes, click the mouse button on the Save Scheme dialog box, or press Tab until the box is highlighted.

4. Click on OK or press Enter. Repeat these steps as necessary for each element you want to change.

This lesson explained how to change screen colors. In the next lesson you'll learn how to work with fonts.

Working with Fonts in the Control Panel

In this lesson, you'll learn how to choose, add, and delete fonts.

The Font option enables you to add or remove fonts within Windows 3. Choosing fonts is a crucial part of creating a document, allowing you to vary the emphasis in your text by using options such as boldface, italics, and different text sizes.

 Font A font is one size and style of a particular typeface. For example, 12-point Times Roman bold is a font.

Not all printers can print a variety of fonts, so you should check your printer's manual to see what types of fonts your printer supports. When you loaded the program, Windows may have installed some fonts for you, based on the printer you selected.

 Point Size The point size of text deals with the heighth of a letter, number, or symbol in a particular typeface.

After you select the Font icon in the Control Panel, the Font window is displayed (see Figure 16-1). Here you can choose a font from the displayed list, add a font, or remove a font.

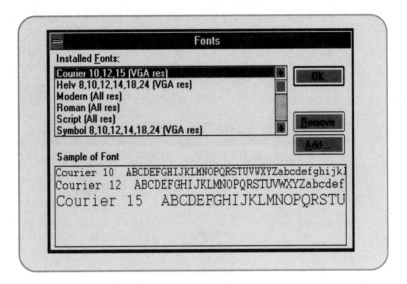

Figure 16-1. The Font window.

Choosing a Font

To choose a font from the list, follow these steps:

1. Use the scroll bars and the pointer or the arrow keys to move through the list until the font you want is highlighted.

2. Click on OK or press Enter.

Adding a Font

You can add fonts to Windows 3 by following these steps:

1. Select the Add button in the Font window. A dialog box lists the font files available (see Figure 16-2).

2. Position the cursor in the Font Filename box and click

91

the mouse button, or press Tab until the box is high-lighted.

3. Type the name and directory of the font file you want to add.

4. Click on OK or press Enter.

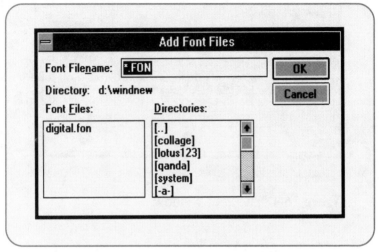

Figure 16-2. The Add Fonts dialog box.

Deleting a Font

To delete a font, follow these steps:

1. In the Font window, highlight the font to remove.

2. Point to or highlight the Remove button.

3. Click the mouse button or press Enter. A screen appears, warning you that a font is about to be deleted.

4. Click on Yes or press Enter.

This lesson introduced fonts. In the next lesson, you'll learn how to further customize your Windows environment.

Customizing with the Control Panel

In this lesson, you'll learn how to customize the mouse, keyboard, sound, and desktop settings.

With the Control Panel, you can customize your mouse, keyboard, the desktop applications, and the use of sound, to set up Windows exactly the way you want.

Customizing Your Mouse

The changes you make affect how quickly your mouse responds when you click the mouse buttons or move the mouse. You can

- Increase the speed of the double-click
- Change the speed of the flashing cursor
- Switch the left/right buttons on your mouse

To open the Mouse application window and make these changes, follow these steps:

1. Point to or highlight the Mouse icon in the Control Panel.

2. Double-click the mouse button or press Enter.

3. Click the mouse button or press Tab to select the options you want to change.

4. Adjust the tracking speed and double-click speed by clicking on the arrows at the end of the setting bar or pressing the left- and right-arrow keys.

Checking Mouse Speed Choose the Test option to test the speed you've chosen.

5. Swap the left and right buttons on the mouse by clicking in the Swap Left/Right buttons box, or by pressing Tab until that box is highlighted and then pressing the space bar.

6. Click on OK or press Enter.

If you change the double-click speed to the fastest setting, the double-click may no longer work. If this happens, reset the double-click speed using the keyboard.

Customizing the Keyboard

The main purpose for the keyboard option is to enable you to change the speed at which keys repeat. To change the keyboard repeat rate, follow these steps:

1. Point to or highlight the Keyboard icon in the Control Panel window.

2. Double-click the mouse button or press Enter.

3. Use the scroll bars or the arrow keys to select the key repeat rate. (To test the key repeat rate, click the mouse button in the Test dialog box or press **T**; then

press and hold any key and Windows shows you the speed you've chosen.)

4. Click on OK or press Enter.

Working with Desktop Applications

You can further customize Windows by changing the way the desktop is displayed. You have the following options:

- The pattern of your screen

- A wallpaper option to enhance what your screen looks like

- The spacing of icons

- The cursor blink rate on-screen

- A sizing grid which enables you to change the borders on your desktop

All of these changes are subjective and will not drastically change the work that you do. Most people, however, have comfort levels for their screen's appearance, the size of the screen, and the spacing of icons within it.

To open and work within the Desktop application, follow these steps:

1. Point to or highlight the Desktop icon.

2. Double-click the mouse button or press Enter. The Desktop window appears.

3. Select the box you want to change.

4. Use the arrow keys or the scroll bars to move through the list of available options until the one you want is highlighted.

5. Click on OK or press Enter.

Customizing the Sound Option

Windows 3 will beep at you when you attempt to do something impossible. You may prefer not to be audibly reprimanded by your computer when you make mistakes. For this reason, Windows gives you the option of turning the beep off. To turn the sound off, follow these steps:

1. Point to or highlight the Sound icon.

2. Double-click the mouse button or press Enter.

3. To turn off the warning beep, click in the box to remove the X, or press Tab to get to the box and press the space bar to remove the X.

4. Click on OK or press Enter.

In this lesson you learned how to customize the Windows environment using the Control Panel. In the next lesson you will be introduced to the printing capabilities in Windows.

Preparing to Print

In this lesson, you'll check your printer setup and get ready to print.

When you first installed Windows, you told the program what type of printer or printers you would be using. Windows then installed a set of instructions—called a *print driver*—that tells the program how to work with the particular printer you have selected.

Checking Printer Setup

Before you print from within Windows, you need to make sure the program is set up to work with your printer. To do this, follow these steps:

1. Select the Control Panel icon from the Main window in the Program Manager.

2. Select the Printers icon. The Printers dialog box is displayed (see Figure 18-1).

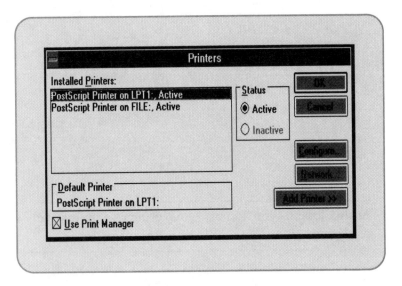

Figure 18-1. The Printers dialog box.

In the Installed Printers box in the upper left corner of the screen, you see the printer or printers you have installed to work with Windows. The Status box shows whether the printer highlighted in the Installed Printers box is active or inactive. (If the printer is selected as active, when you print, text will be printed on that printer.)

If Your Printer Doesn't Print Properly When you print, if things don't come out the way you expected, return to the Printers dialog box and make sure that (1) the printer you are trying to use is selected as the active printer and (2) that the correct printer driver is selected for your printer. (If you are unsure about which printer driver works with your printer, consult your printer's manual.)

The next step involves checking the way your printer is connected.

● Click on the Configure button in the Printers dialog box. The Printers Configure dialog box is displayed (see Figure 18-2).

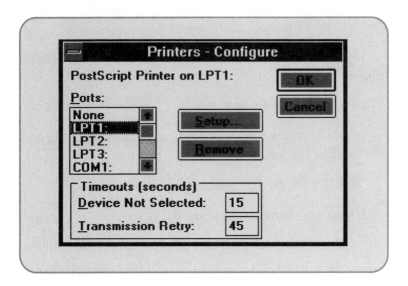

Figure 18-2. The Printers Configure dialog box.

This dialog box shows you which port your printer is connected to and displays additional settings that control the timing of the data sent to the printer. You need to be concerned only with the selected port. Usually your printer will be connected to LPT1 or LPT2 (for a parallel printer) or COM1 (for a serial printer).

Printer Port The port your printer is connected to is the outlet on the back of your computer to which your printer is attached. The data is sent from the computer to the printer through a cable attached to the port.

Parallel and Serial Printers The terms *parallel printer* and *serial printer* relate to the way data is sent from the computer to the printer. If you are unsure which type of printer you have, consult your printer's manual or contact the printer's manufacturer.

If you need to select a different port for your printer, follow these steps.

If you are using a mouse:

1. Position the mouse pointer on the port you need and click the mouse button.

2. Click on the OK button.

If you are using the keyboard:

1. Press Tab until the Ports box is selected and then use the arrow keys to highlight the port you need.

2. Press Enter.

You are then returned to the Printers dialog box. To exit, click on the OK button, or press Tab until the OK button is selected and press Enter.

In this lesson you learned how to get ready to print. The next lesson introduces you to printing with Windows Print Manager.

Lesson 19

Printing with the Print Manager

In this lesson, you'll learn how to print from within Windows by using the Windows Print Manager.

The Print Manager is a utility within Windows that controls and prints the files you send from the computer to the printer. Because the Print Manager takes care of sending and printing the files, you can continue your work in Windows applications without waiting for the file to be printed.

Note: Although all Windows 3 applications use the Print Manager to send and print files, the way you start the printing process from within the application may vary slightly from program to program. For example, if you are using Windows Write, you start printing by opening the file you want to print, and selecting the Print option from the File menu. The Print Manager then takes over the process of sending the file to the printer.

Looking at the Print Queue

When you print files, Windows creates a print queue—a listing of files that are being sent to the printer, in the order you

101

selected. You can display the Print Manager's print queue and modify the order, pause and resume printing, and also delete a file from the print queue.

Before you can display the files currently in the print queue, you must select files to be printed. You do this from within the Windows application you are using. (You may need to consult your applications manual in order to find out specifically how to do this.) In most Windows applications, you start the print process by selecting the **Print** option from the File menu. Once you've started the printing process, the Print Manager takes over.

After you've done this, you can go into the Print Manager and look at the files in the print queue. To display the print queue, follow these steps:

1. Open the Main window in the Program Manager.

2. Select the Print Manager icon.

The Print Manager window is then displayed (see Figure 19-1). In this window, you see a menu bar, and, if you've sent a file (or files) to the printer, a message box telling you which file is currently printing to which printer, and information about each of the files you have selected to be printed.

The files are numbered according to the order in which they are to be printed. The small computer icon beside the topmost file shows you that this file is currently being printed.

Changing Print Order

After you've displayed the print queue, you can change the order of the files you are printing. To move the placement of a file in the print queue, follow these steps:

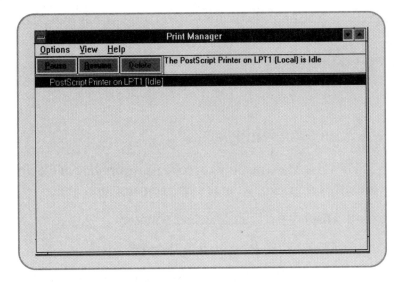

Figure 19-1. Displaying the print queue.

1. Point to the file you want to move or use Tab and the arrow keys to move the highlight to the file.

2. Using a mouse, drag the file to the point in the queue at which you want the file to be printed. Using the keyboard, press Ctrl and then the up- or down-arrow keys to move the file. (For example, if the file is fourth in the print queue and you want to move it to the second position, move the file up into the spot currently occupied by the second file in the print queue.)

3. Release the mouse button, or release Ctrl and the arrow key you were using.

Windows then renumbers the files in the queue and will print the files in the new order.

Changing the Order of the Current File Windows will not allow you to change the order of a file that is currently printing. You can pause or cancel printing of the current file, however, and then reorder the queue as necessary.

Pausing Printing

The Print Manager allows you to pause printing of the file currently being sent to the printer. To pause printing,

1. Display the Print Manager window.

2. Click on the Pause button or press Alt+P.

The message box shows you that printing has been paused for the current file (see Figure 19-2).

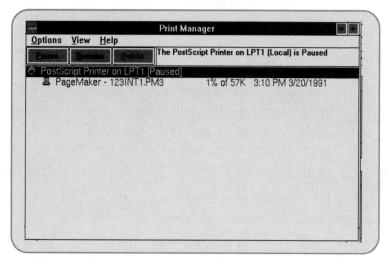

Figure 19-2. Pausing printing of the current file.

Resuming Printing

When you want to resume printing of the current file, follow these steps:

1. Make sure that the file you want to resume printing on is still selected.

2. Click on the Resume button or press Alt+R.

Resuming Printing If your laser printer stalls during printing, press Alt+R.

Deleting Items from the Print Queue

In some cases, you may want to cancel printing of a particular file before it is printed. For example, suppose that after you initiate printing of a document, you realize that there are some last-minute changes you need to make.

To delete a file from the print queue, follow these steps:

1. Choose the file you want to delete.

2. Click on the Delete button or press Alt+D. Windows then asks you whether you want to proceed with deleting the file.

3. Click on OK or press Enter.

Deleting All Print Queue Files Sometimes, you may want to delete all the files you've sent to the Print Manager. To do this, simply open the Options menu in the Print Manager window and choose the **Exit** option. Then click on OK or press Enter to cancel the Print Manager's queue.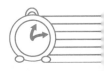

In this lesson, you learned to initiate printing from within applications and control the way files are printed by using the Print Manager. In the next lesson you'll learn how to work with Windows Write.

Using Windows Write

In this lesson, you'll learn to start and exit Windows Write and create a simple document.

Starting Windows Write

Windows Write is a word processing program that comes with your version of Windows 3. You can use Windows Write to produce memos, letters, reports, and various other types of business or personal correspondence.

To start Windows Write, follow these steps:

1. From the Program Manager window, select the Accessories icon.

2. From the Accessories group window, select the Write icon.

The Windows Write screen is then displayed (see Figure 20-1). At the top of the Write screen you see the name of the application and the word *(untitled)*, which indicates that this is a new file that has not yet been saved.

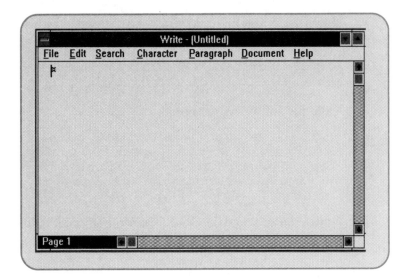

Figure 20-1. The Windows Write screen.

The menu bar contains all the menus and options you will use as you work with documents in Windows Write. Scroll bars allow you to display different parts of the documents you create. Like other windows, you can make the window smaller or larger or reduce it to an icon.

At the top of the work area of the window you see the text cursor. This cursor marks the point where text will be inserted when you begin typing.

Entering Text

To enter text in Windows Write, try typing the following example.

1. Type the following line:

```
Dear Ms. Morris,
```

2. Press Enter twice.

When you press Enter the first time, the cursor moves to the line below the text you typed. When you press Enter again, the cursor moves down another line, which leaves a blank line after the text.

3. Type the following paragraph:

   Thank you for your hospitality over the holidays. We really enjoyed our stay in New York and are confident that the proposals we discussed will benefit both companies mutually.

   Notice that as you type, Windows Write automatically moves to the second line when the first line of text is full. This is known as word wrap.

4. Press Enter. The document should now appear similar to the one shown in Figure 20-2.

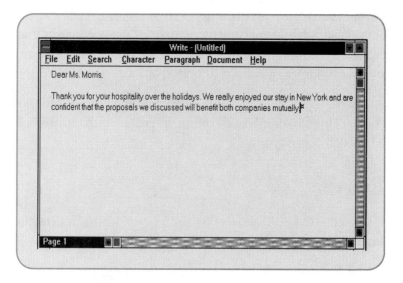

Figure 20-2. The sample document.

Moving Around in the Document

If you are using a mouse, you can move the cursor by positioning the mouse pointer where you want the cursor, and clicking the mouse button. Try these steps:

1. Position the mouse pointer after the word *Morris* and click the mouse button.

2. Move the mouse pointer to the word *benefit* and click the mouse button.

If you are using the keyboard, Table 20-1 highlights the keys that will enable you to place the cursor where you want it.

Table 20-1. Keys Used To Move the Cursor in Windows Write

Key	Moves the Cursor
Down arrow	Down one line
Up arrow	Up one line
Right arrow	Right one character
Left arrow	Left one character
PgUp	To the previous screen
PgDn	To the next screen
Ctrl-Right arrow	To the next word
Ctrl-Left arrow	To the previous word
Ctrl-PgUp	To top of the screen
Ctrl-PgDn	To bottom of the screen
Home	To the start of line
End	To the end of line
Ctrl-Home	To the start of document
Ctrl-End	To the end of document

Selecting Text

Before you can work with the text you have entered, you have to know how to select it. The way you select text depends on whether you are using the mouse or the keyboard.

Using a Mouse To Select Text

To select text using a mouse, follow these steps.

1. Position the mouse pointer at the start of the text you want to select.

2. Drag the mouse until the section you want is highlighted.

3. Release the mouse button.

Selecting a Paragraph You can select an entire paragraph by positioning the mouse pointer to the left of the paragraph you want and double-clicking the mouse button (see Figure 20-3).

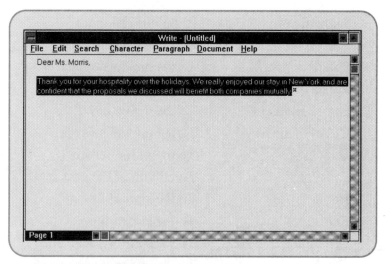

Figure 20-3. Selecting a paragraph.

110

Windows 3 gives you a shortcut to selecting text: You can use the space to the left of the text (called the selection area) to highlight portions of text.

For example, to select the first line of text in the document:

1. Position the mouse pointer to the left of the first line.

2. Click the mouse button.

Selecting Multiple Lines of Text You can use the selection area to select additional lines of text by clicking in the selection area and dragging the mouse downward until the section you want is highlighted.

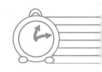

Using the Keyboard To Select Text

Use the cursor-movement keys explained in Table 20-1 to position the cursor at the point you want to begin highlighting. Then press Shift and move the cursor to the point where you want highlighting to end.

Selecting an Entire Document If you are using the keyboard, you can select an entire document by moving to the beginning of the document (Ctrl+Home), pressing Shift, and moving to the end of the document (Ctrl+End).

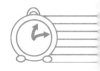

Unselecting Text

You can remove the highlight from text you've selected one of two ways.

If you are using a mouse:

1. Move the mouse pointer into the work area of the screen.

111

2. Click the mouse button.

If you are using the keyboard:

1. Release the Shift key.

2. Press one of the cursor-movement keys.

Working with Selected Text

Now that you've got the text selected, you can copy, cut, paste, or change the style of the text. You can make the text boldfaced, italic, or change the way the text is aligned on the page. All of these options are available in the menus displayed in the menu bar at the top of the Write work area.

To show how you can work with selected text, try a basic move procedure.

1. Select the portion of text you want to move.

2. Open the Edit menu.

3. Choose Cut.

Windows Write places the selected text on the clipboard. You can then paste the text anywhere in the document by following these steps:

1. Use the mouse or the keyboard to move the cursor to the point where you want to paste the text.

2. Open the Edit menu.

3. Choose the Paste option.

Write places the text at the position you indicated. Experiment with the other menu bar options for selected text. Remember, if you change your mind about any menu, you can close it by clicking outside it.

Printing the Document

Once you write and refine your Windows Write document, you'll probably want to print it. To print your document, follow these steps:

1. Open the File menu and choose the Print option. The Print dialog box, shown in Figure 20-4, is displayed.

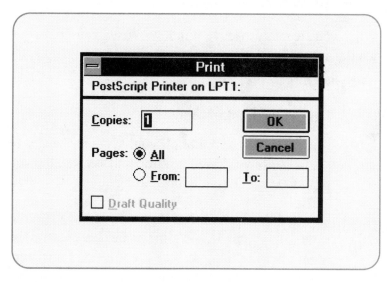

Figure 20-4. The Print dialog box.

2. Type the number of copies you want.

3. Select whether you want to print all of the document or only selected pages. (If you want to select a specific range of pages to print, enter the starting page number in the From box and the ending page number in the To box.)

4. Click on the OK button or press Enter. Windows then prints the document.

What If Your Document Didn't Print? If your document didn't print or Windows displayed an error, check to make sure your printer is set up correctly. (For more information on setting up your printer to print from within Windows applications, see Lesson 18.)

Exiting Windows Write

When you are ready to leave Windows Write, you exit as you would any application.

1. Save the file you've been working on.

2. Display the Control menu.

3. Choose the Close option. If you've made changes to the file since you saved it, Write will ask whether you want to save the file before exiting.

 Saving Files If you have previously saved a file and want to save it under the same name or are saving the file for the first time, select **Save** from the File menu. If you want to save the file under a different name, choose **Save As**.

4. Click on OK to save the file or Cancel to stop the save procedure and exit.

You are then returned to the Program Manager.

In this lesson, you learned some of the basics of using Windows Write. In the next lesson, you'll explore another add-in feature of Windows 3: Windows Paintbrush.

Lesson 21

Using Windows Paintbrush

In this lesson, you'll learn how to create drawings with Windows Paintbrush.

Starting Windows Paintbrush

Windows Paintbrush is another add-in program with Windows 3 that enables you to create artwork you can include in other Windows applications.

To start Windows Paintbrush, follow these steps.

If you are using a mouse:

1. From the Program Manager window, double-click on the Accessories icon.

2. Position the mouse pointer on the Paintbrush icon and double-click the mouse button.

If you are using the keyboard:

1. In the Program Manager window, use the arrow keys to move the highlight to the Accessories icon; then press Enter.

2. Move the highlight to the Paintbrush icon and press Enter.

The Paintbrush screen is then displayed (see Figure 21-1). At the top of the screen you see the name of the application and the word *(untitled)*, which indicates that this is a new file that has not yet been saved.

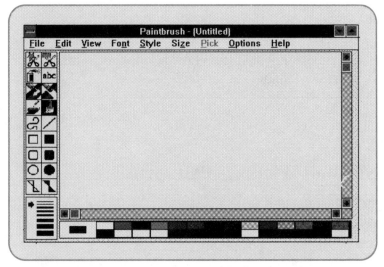

Figure 21-1. The Windows Paintbrush screen.

Although all Windows applications have the same basic look, the Paintbrush screen is a little different. Close to the top of the window, you see the familiar menu bar. Along the left edge of the screen, a double row of drawing tools is displayed (see Figure 21-2). At the bottom of the window, a color palette offers you a variety of colors and patterns for filling shapes and coloring the background and foreground of your drawings. At the right edge of the screen is the traditional scroll bar, enabling you to move through the drawing you create.

Learning To Draw

If you are using a mouse, drawing with Windows Paintbrush is as easy as moving your hand. You simply select a drawing tool, choose a line width and a color from the color palette, position the mouse pointer where you want to begin drawing, press the mouse button, and draw.

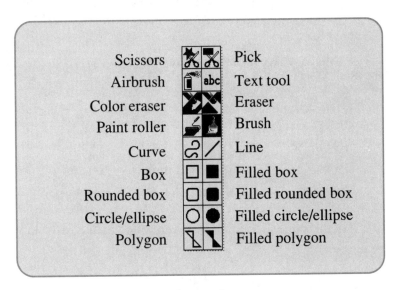

Scissors		Pick
Airbrush		Text tool
Color eraser		Eraser
Paint roller		Brush
Curve		Line
Box		Filled box
Rounded box		Filled rounded box
Circle/ellipse		Filled circle/ellipse
Polygon		Filled polygon

Figure 21-2. The drawing tools.

Try drawing with a few simple exercises.

1. Move the mouse pointer over to the tools row.

2. Click on the filled box tool.

3. Move the mouse pointer to the middle of the work area.

4. Press and hold the mouse button and drag the mouse down and to the right. Windows Paintbrush draws a box.

5. Release the mouse button. Paintbrush fills the box with the color you selected at the bottom of the screen. (You can tell which color or pattern is selected by the selection shown to the left of the palette.)

If you're using the keyboard, drawing is a little different. In this case, you need to remember some special keys you'll use to emulate mouse operations. Table 21-1 shows which keys to press when you're using Windows Paintbrush.

Table 21-1. Keys Used in Drawing

Key	Operation
Insert	Press left mouse button
F9+Insert	Double-click left mouse button
Delete	Press right mouse button
F9+Delete	Double-click right mouse button

Try the same procedure just mentioned by using the keyboard.

1. Use the arrow keys to move the mouse pointer over to the tools row.

2. Position the pointer on the filled box tool and press Insert.

3. Use the arrow keys to move the mouse pointer to the middle of the work area.

4. Press and hold the Insert key and use the right- and down-arrow keys to expand the box.

5. Release the Insert key.

Selecting a Background

Windows Paintbrush gives you the option of selecting a background color or pattern for your drawings. The Selected Colors box, shown at the left end of the palette row, displays the colors currently selected. The outside of the box (shown in Figure 21-1 as white) shows the color selected for the background; the inside of the box (shown as black) represents the color chosen for the foreground.

> **Background** The background of your drawing is the work area space on which you draw graphics. White is the background color selected when you start Windows Paintbrush.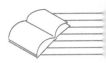

To select a background, follow these steps:

1. Move the pointer to the color or pattern you want in the palette row. Using the keyboard, press Tab to get to the palette and use the arrow keys to move to the color or pattern.

2. Click the right mouse button or press Delete.

The new background is displayed in the Selected Colors box.

Selecting a Foreground

> **Foreground** The foreground of your drawing is the color or pattern used when you add shapes, lines, and other art items on top of the background. The default color for the foreground is black.

To select a new foreground color, follow these steps:

1. Move the pointer to the color or pattern you want in the palette row. Using the keyboard, press Tab to get

119

to the palette and use the arrow keys to move to the color or pattern.

2. Click the left mouse button or press Delete. The new color is then shown in the Selected Colors box.

Using Drawing Tools

When you first start Windows Paintbrush, the brush tool is the tool initially selected. You can use the brush tool or select another tool before you begin drawing or at any time you are working on the art you create.

Selecting a Drawing Tool

To select a drawing tool, follow these steps:

1. Move the mouse pointer to the tool you want to select or use the arrow keys to move the pointer to the tool you want (in this case, choose the circle tool.)

2. Click the mouse button or press Insert.

Paintbrush then makes that tool the selected tool.

Drawing with Art Tools

After you've selected a tool, you're ready to draw something on-screen. To use a drawing tool, follow these steps:

1. Use the mouse or the arrow keys to move the pointer to the point on-screen where you want to begin drawing.

2. Press and hold the mouse button or the Insert key.

3. Use the mouse or the arrow keys to move the pointer in the direction you want to draw. (Remember to keep

the mouse button or the Insert key pressed while you do this.) When you are using a tool that draws an object like a box or a circle, the shape grows and shrinks as you move the cursor.

4. When you're finished drawing, release the mouse button or the Insert key. Figure 21-3 shows an example of a circle drawn in this exercise.

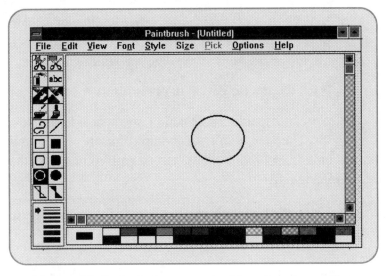

Figure 21-3. A circle created with a drawing tool.

Take a few minutes and experiment with the different drawing tools.

I Wish I Hadn't Done That... When you add an art element that doesn't look right or didn't turn out the way you'd intended, you can remove it by using the Undo feature. Undo the last addition you made by opening the Edit menu and choosing **Undo** or by pressing Alt-Backspace.

Choosing Line Width

Paintbrush also allows you to choose the line thickness of the objects you draw. For example, you may want to thicken the border used when you draw with the rectangle tool. Paintbrush shows you the current line width in the Linesize box located in the lower left corner of the screen.

To change the line width, follow these steps:

1. Move the mouse pointer to the line width you want to select, or press Tab to get to the Linesize box and then use the arrow keys to move to the width you want.

2. Click the mouse button or press Insert.

Paintbrush displays the selection arrow beside the new line width. The new width will be used for all objects you draw—circles, polygons, lines, etc.—until you change the line width again.

 Using the Eraser You can use the Eraser tool to erase unwanted items on the screen.

Viewing a Drawing

Paintbrush enables you to display your drawing in several different ways. The regular display, which is the default when you start Paintbrush, shows you only a portion of the actual page. You can also zoom the screen out to display the entire page, or you can remove the drawing tools and the palette to display only your drawing in the actual screen. Particularly important when you want to edit your drawing, the zoom-in feature allows you to get a close-up look at (and edit) the individual dots that make up your drawing.

Zooming Out

To zoom out the display to see the entire page, follow these steps:

1. Open the View menu.

2. Choose the Zoom Out option.

The screen then displays the entire page (your drawing will look much smaller than it did in the original screen).

To return to the normal screen,

1. Open the View menu.

2. Choose Zoom In.

The screen is returned to its normal display.

Maximizing the Work Area

To remove the tools and the color palette to get the maximum display area on-screen, follow these steps:

1. Open the View menu.

2. Choose the View Picture option.

The tools row and the palette are removed, displaying only your drawing in the work area. Note, however, that you cannot edit your drawing while the tools and the palette are missing from the screen. To return to the normal display, click the mouse button or press Esc.

Zooming In

Earlier in this lesson, you used **Zoom In** to reverse the full-page display you created by selecting **Zoom Out**. You can also use the **Zoom In** option to magnify your drawing and work with the individual dots (called *pixels*) that make up the artwork.

To zoom in, follow these steps:

1. Open the View menu.

2. Choose the Zoom In option.

3. Place the box at the point you want to magnify and click the mouse button or press Enter.

Paintbrush then displays the drawing magnified several times its normal size. You can then edit the pixels by changing color, adding or deleting them, or erasing them. To return to normal display, open the View menu and choose **Zoom Out**.

Starting Over You can clear the screen by pressing Ctrl+N or selecting **New** from the File menu.

Saving Paintbrush Files

Remember to save your work periodically, so a badly timed thunderstorm doesn't erase everything you've done. To save your Paintbrush drawing, follow these steps:

1. Open the File menu.

2. Choose the Save option.

3. Position the cursor in the appropriate box and type a file name for the drawing.

4. Click on the OK button or press Enter.

Exiting Windows Paintbrush

When you are ready to exit Paintbrush, follow these steps:

1. Open the File menu.

2. Choose Exit.

If you haven't saved your drawing, Paintbrush asks you to confirm that you want to exit without saving. If you haven't made any changes, you are returned to the Program Manager.

In this lesson, you learned some of the basics of Windows Paintbrush. In the next lesson you will learn how to work with the desktop accessories.

Using Desktop Accessories

In this lesson, you will learn how to work in the Accessories window using the Notepad, Cardfile, Calendar, Calculator, and Clock.

Opening the Accessories Window

When you first start Windows 3, the Accessories window will be shown as a group icon in the lower portion of the screen. To open the Accessories window, follow these steps:

1. Use the pointer or Ctrl+Tab to highlight the Accessories icon.

2. Double-click the mouse button or press Enter.

The Accessories window is available anytime you are working in Windows 3 (see Figure 22-1). The following applications are available:

● Write

● Paintbrush

● Terminal

● Notepad

- Recorder

- Cardfile

- Calendar

- Calculator

- Clock

- PIF Editor

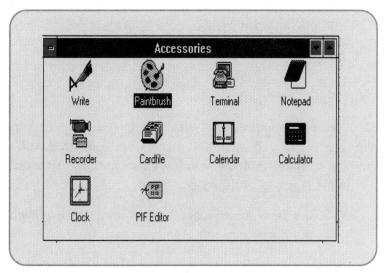

Figure 22-1. The Accessories window.

The Accessories window allows you to perform simple applications while other programs are running. If, for example, you are working in the File Manager and need to make a note to yourself regarding a deadline, you can

1. Open the Accessories window.

2. Choose the Notepad application.

3. Enter your reminder while the File Manager is still running.

127

Working with the Accessories

This lesson introduces you to several of the most popular accessories you will use during your work with Windows. For more information on the accessories not covered here, see *The Best Book of Microsoft Windows 3.*

After you open the Accessories window, you can choose the application you want:

1. Use the pointer or the arrow keys to highlight the application you want.

2. Double-click the mouse button or press Enter.

Using the Notepad

The Notepad application is like a mini word processor, allowing you to jot down notes, memos, and reminders while you are working in other Windows applications. To work within the Notepad, follow these steps:

1. Select the Notepad icon. A blank screen is displayed with a flashing cursor in the top left corner.

2. Type your information, pressing Enter at the end of each line, such as

   ```
   1:00PM    10/23/90

   Had lunch with John Smith, corporate ex-
   ecutive from XYZ Widget Company. Set up
   order schedule for 1991.
   ```

3. Save the information by choosing the Save command from the File menu.

4. The File Save As window appears, asking you to type in a file name. Type Widget91 in the dialog box.

5. Choose OK.

This example allows you to enter and save text in the Notepad. Within the Notepad you can also print, edit, and get help with text you are working with.

Using the Cardfile

The Cardfile is an application in the Accessories window that functions very much like a Rolodex. You can use the Cardfile to keep track of names, addresses, and phone numbers. Suppose, for example, you wanted to enter John Smith's address and phone number into your Cardfile. To do this, follow these steps:

1. Select the Cardfile icon. You will see a blank screen with a flashing cursor in the top left corner.

2. Open the Edit menu.

3. Choose the Index option. An Index Line dialog box is displayed so that you can name the index card (see Figure 22-2).

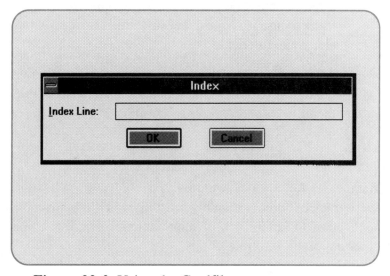

Figure 22-2. Using the Cardfile.

4. Type **John Smith** and press Enter. The flashing cursor appears back in the information window.

5. Type the following information, pressing Enter after each line:

```
1023 Acacia Rd.
Chicago IL 60623
(604)891-2323
```

Within the Cardfile you can edit information, view your data in either card or list form, add cards, delete cards, and search for a particular cardfile. You can also use the help menu if you are having problems.

After the necessary information you have entered in the Cardfile, you need to save the list of cards you have created. Here's how:

1. Open the File menu.

2. Choose the **Save** option.

3. Type a name for the Cardfile (in this case, you might want to use **Rolodex**, because this list acts as an electronic rolodex).

4. After you've saved the cards, return to the Accessories window by choosing the **Exit** command from the File menu.

Using the Calendar

Within the Accessories window, the Calendar application keeps track of daily or monthly scheduling. You can use this application to keep track of appointments, deadlines, and other important information.

After the Calendar is opened, you can view it in daily or monthly form. The Calendar also has an alarm that you can set so that you don't forget important appointments. Suppose, for example, you have another important lunch appointment with John Smith of XYZ Widget Co. on the 30th of this month at 12:00PM. To enter this information into your calendar, follow these steps:

1. From the View menu choose the Month command or press F9 on the keyboard.

2. Use the pointer or the arrow keys to highlight the 30th day on the calendar.

3. Press Enter.

4. A daily calendar for the 30th is displayed.

5. Position the flashing cursor after 12:00PM.

6. Type in the following information:

   `Lunch with John Smith: XYZ Widgets`

7. To make sure that you don't forget, choose the Set command from the Alarm menu while the cursor is on the 12:00PM line. A small bell will appear before 12:00PM activating the alarm for that time (see Figure 22-3). If you want to remove the alarm, repeat this step.

8. Open the File menu.

9. Choose Save and a dialog box appears so that you can enter a file name.

10. Type the name you want to use for the calendar.

11. Choose OK or press Enter.

12. To exit the Calendar, choose the Exit option from the File menu.

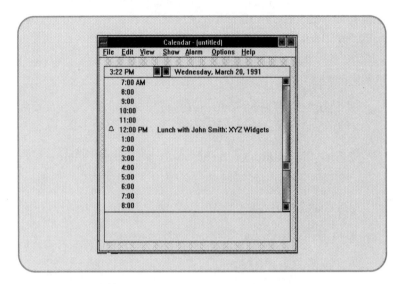

Figure 22-3. Setting an alarm for an appointment.

In the Calendar application you can enter or delete information as frequently as you like. You can also edit data and get help from the Help menu if you are having difficulties.

Using the Calculator

The Calculator application works just like a normal desktop calculator. You can use the calculator in either standard or scientific form, depending on the complexity of your work. To move around in the calculator

● Use the mouse pointer and click the mouse button.

Or

● Use the keys on the keyboard that correspond to the functions on-screen.

To switch back and forth from the scientific and standard modes, use the View menu. To learn more about the complex functions available, refer to the Windows 3.0 users manual.

Suppose that you need to know what ((1286) * (472)) is for an important accounting function. From the standard mode in the calculator, follow these steps:

1. Make sure the Num Lock light on your keyboard is on.

2. Type 1286. (Notice that the numbers appear in the dialog box as you type them.)

3. Now press Shift-*, or place the pointer on the multiplication symbol and click the mouse button.

4. Type 472.

5. Place the pointer over the equals sign and click the mouse button, or press = on the keyboard and the answer appears in the dialog box.

Using the Clock

The Clock application helps you keep track of time while you are working in Windows 3. When you installed Windows, the clock was set to the correct time. You can view the clock in either digital or analog mode. To change the mode of the clock, follow these steps:

1. Open the Settings menu.

2. Choose the Analog or Digital option.

If you need to reset the clock, you can do so from the Control Panel. If you want to keep the clock on-screen while you are working, choose **Minimize** from the Control menu and the clock will shrink to icon size.

Exiting the Accessories Window

After you have finished working in the Accessories window, you need to return to the Main menu screen or to another application you are working with. To exit the Accessories window, follow these steps:

1. Open the Control menu in the top left corner of the screen.

2. Choose the Close command.

In this lesson, you learned about several of the most often-used applications in the Accessories window.

With the end of this lesson, you've completed your *10 Minute Guide to Windows 3*. At the back of this book, you'll find a "DOS Primer" that introduces you to several of the basic DOS commands you'll use in a typical worksession.

Windows 3 Table of Features

Feature	Description	To Start
Real mode	Allows users to run non-Windows applications; also allows users with limited memory to run Windows	Add /r after WIN at startup; as in WIN/r
Standard mode	Runs Windows at maximum configuration possible on user's machine	Type WIN and press Enter
Enhanced mode	Allows users to take full advantage of their 386 systems within Windows	Add /3 after WIN at startup; as in WIN/3
Network mode	Allows users to run Windows in a network environment	Specify network setup at installation
Program Manager	Controls the graphic interface of Windows; allows users to open and work with applications by selecting icons and options	The Program Manager is started automatically whenever Windows is active
File Manager	Enables users to work with files easily; has basic operations for file maintenance and organization	From within the Main group window, select the File Manager icon
Directory Tree	A feature of the File Manager that displays directories and files in tree form	The Directory Tree is automatically displayed when the File Manager is started
Print Manager	Organizes and takes over printing of files; places print files in a print queue that users can manipulate and modify	From the Main group window, select the Print Manager icon

Feature	Description	To Start
Control Panel	Provides users with options for customizing Windows;	From the Main group window, select the Control Panel icon
Calendar	Lets users maintain a calendar of appointments and events; can display in either daily or monthly form	From the Accessories group window, select the Calendar icon
Calculator	Enables users to use the numeric keypad like a desktop calculator	From the Accessories group window, select the Calculator icon
Cardfile	Helps users organize and maintain information in the form of a Rolodex file	From the Accessories group window, select the Cardfile icon
Notepad	Enables users to compose notes and memos without leaving Windows	From the Accessories group window, select the Notepad icon
Terminal	A communications program that lets users connect with and transfer files to and from remote computers	From the Accessories group window, select the Terminal icon
Windows Write	A word processing program that runs under Windows	From the Accessories window, select the Write icon
Windows Paintbrush	A drawing program that enables users to create graphics	From the Accessories window, select the Paintbrush icon
Windows Recorder	A macro feature that helps users streamline procedures they use often	From the Accessories window, select the Recorder icon
PIF File Editor	A feature that allows users to set up files to control the execution of non-Windows programs running under Windows	From the Main window, select the Accessories icon; then choose the PIF Editor icon

DOS Primer

This section highlights some of the DOS procedures you will use during your work with Microsoft Windows and other programs.

Preparing Disks

The first step in preparing disks to store programs and data is formatting the disks.

What Is Formatting? The formatting procedure writes important information to the disk, preparing it to store data. You cannot place any information—programs or data of any kind—on a new disk before the disk is formatted. Formatting also erases any information on a diskette. *Do not* format your hard disk drive, however, because formatting a hard disk erases all programs and information on the hard disk.

1. Turn the computer on.

2. If the system asks you for the date and time, type these in and press Enter after each entry. (Not all systems ask for the date and time.) Enter the date in the form MM:DD:YY (such as 11:23:90) and the time in the form HH:MM:SS (such as 08:30:00).

3. Change to the drive and directory that contains your DOS files. For example, if your DOS files are in C:\DOS, type cd\ DOS at the C> prompt and press Enter.

4. Insert the first blank disk in the A: or B: drive and close the drive door.

5. Type FORMAT A: or FORMAT B: and press Enter. The system will tell you to insert the disk (which you've already done).

6. Press Enter. The system then begins formatting the disk. When the format is complete, the system asks whether you want to format another.

7. Type Y. If you want to format additional disks, then repeat these steps. Type N if you do not want to format disks.

Labeling Disks While the disk is being formatted, you may want to use the time to write the labels for the disks. Be sure to write on the labels before you attach them to the diskettes. (If you've already placed the labels on the diskettes, write on the labels using a felt-tip pen. The hard point of a ball-point pen can damage the surface of a diskette.)

Repeat these steps as many times as necessary to format the disks. Now you can make a backup copy of your Windows program.

Making Backup Copies

To make a copy of your Windows program, follow these steps:

1. Place the original Windows disk in drive A.

2. Place the blank, formatted disk to which you want to copy in drive B.

3. Type **DISKCOPY A: B:** and press Enter. (If you have two drives that are different sizes—such as one 5.25 and one 3.5 inch drive—or you have only one floppy drive, use **DISKCOPY A: A:** instead.)

The system then copies to drive B the information from the disk in drive A. When the operation is complete, the system asks whether you want to copy another disk.

4. Type **Y**.

DOS Confusion If you're having trouble under-standing some of these commands, don't worry—the formatting and copying procedures are part of DOS, your computer's operating system.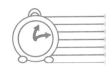

Repeat the DISKCOPY procedure until you've copied all your Windows disks. Now you're ready to install the program (see inside front cover).

Working with Directories

DOS enables you to organize your files in directories and sub-directories. You can think of this organization as a tree struc-ture—each directory can have subdirectories (like the branches splitting off the trunk of a tree).

Making Directories

To create a directory, use the **MD** (Make Directory) com-mand. Follow these steps:

1. At the DOS prompt, type **MD** *drive:\directoryname*.

In this example, substitute the name for the directory you are creating in place of *directoryname*.

2. Press Enter.

This command causes DOS to create the directory under the name you specified and on the drive you specified.

 Root Directory The root directory is the main directory on your disk (the trunk of the tree). All other directories and subdirectories are divisions of the root directory.

Note: You do not need to create a directory in order to run Windows; the installation program takes care of this for you. You may want to create additional directories to store your data files, however.

Moving to a Directory

You need to be able to move from directory to directory. To change directories, use the CD (Change Directory) command:

1. At the DOS prompt, type **CD** \ *directoryname*.

In this command line, the backslash (\) tells DOS to begin at the root directory and move to the directory you specified under the root. You use the backslash to separate all directories and subdirectories in a command line. For example, if you wanted to move to a subdirectory of the directory shown above, the command line would look like this:

```
CD \directoryname\subdirectoryname
```

2. Press Enter.

DOS then moves to the directory or subdirectory you specified.

Displaying Directory Contents

To see which files are stored in a directory, use the command DIR (Directory):

1. Change to the directory you want to display.

2. Type **DIR**.

3. Press Enter.

DOS then displays a list of all the files in the current directory.

Working with Files

DOS also includes commands you can use to work with the files you create. This section briefly introduces the procedures for copying, deleting, and renaming files.

Copying Files

When you want to copy files using DOS, use the COPY command:

1. Move to the directory that stores the file (or files) you want to copy.

2. Type the command line

   ```
   COPY filename1 filename2
   ```

In this command line, *filename1* is the name of the existing file you want to copy, and *filename2* is the new name you want the copy of the file to be given. If you want to copy the file to a different drive or directory, specify the path before *filename*.

141

3. Press Enter.

DOS then copies the file and places the copy in the current directory.

Deleting Files

When you delete files using DOS, use the ERASE (or DEL) command:

1. Move to the directory that stores the file you want to erase.

2. Type the command line

   `ERASE filename`

   Or

   `DEL filename`

3. Press Enter.

4. When DOS asks you for confirmation, type Y.

DOS then deletes the file.

Renaming Files

Use the RENAME (or REN) command to rename files in DOS:

1. Move to the directory that stores the file you want to rename.

2. Type the command line

   `RENAME filename1 filename2`

   Or

   `REN filename1 filename2`

In this command line, *filename1* is the name of the existing file, and *filename2* is the new name you want to assign to the file.

3. Press Enter.

DOS then renames the file and keeps it in the current directory.

For more information about using DOS commands, see *The First Book of MS-DOS.*

Index